HE WAS THE LESSON, I AM THE STORY

Unmasking What Was Unseen,
Reclaiming What Was Mine

Tanya T. Bennett, BSN, RN

HE WAS THE LESSON, I AM THE STORY:

Unmasking What Was Unseen, Reclaiming What Was Mine

by

Tanya T. Bennett, BSN, RN

For permission requests, contact:

PUSH 365 EVENT GROUP LLC

Email: info@push365eventgroup.com

ISBN: 979-8-218-86948-9

Cover and author photos by Evan Marcus Imagery.

Cover design by Autographx Creative Agency.

Published by PUSH 365 Event Group LLC

Chicago, Illinois

DISCLAIMER

***

This is a work of nonfiction based on the author's personal experiences. Some names and identifying details have been changed to protect privacy. In certain cases, composite characters have been created or timelines condensed to preserve confidentiality and maintain narrative flow. The goal in all cases is to protect individuals' privacy without compromising the integrity of the story. The events are portrayed to the best of the author's memory and reflection.

Under no circumstances will any blame, liability, or legal responsibility be held against the author or publisher for any damages, reparations, or monetary loss resulting directly or indirectly from the information contained within this work.

DEDICATION

***

For my mother, your unwavering love and quiet wisdom anchored me through every storm and reminded me that grace can be steady and soft at the same time.

For my father, though you are no longer here, your lessons and laughter echo through my choices and continue to guide my steps.

For my daughter, Tylar, my heartbeat, my why, and my constant reminder that love multiplies when it is nurtured in truth.

For my brother, Terrell, and my sister-in-love, Dominique, your laughter and loyalty remind me daily that family is both chosen and blood-bound.

And for every woman who has ever lost herself in love only to find her way back stronger, may these pages remind you that healing does not erase the story, it rewrites the ending.

—Tanya

ACKNOWLEDGMENTS

***

This book exists because of a village filled with love, patience, and faith.

To my family and friends, your support lifted me when I wanted to surrender. Your belief in me brought these pages to life.

To my sister circle, thank you for the prayers, the laughter, and the late-night talks that reminded me I was always supported. You each show me grace lived out loud.

To my closest male friends, you demonstrated that strength and gentleness can exist together, and that protection and respect are inseparable.

To all my exes, I appreciate the lessons that fueled my growth. Heartbreak became the foundation for wisdom, boundaries, and a deeper self-love.

To my therapists and life coach, whose wisdom and support helped me untangle what I carried and taught me to name truth without shame, this story bears your fingerprints in every healed sentence.

To my PUSH 365 and HFCC community, your inspiration keeps purpose at the center of everything I build, and your stories show how sharing can change culture.

To every reader who finds herself in these pages, may you be met with comfort and a reminder that your healing matters and is sacred.

A NOTE BEFORE YOU BEGIN

***

This memoir is inspired by true events. While some names, details, and circumstances have been altered or blended to protect privacy, the emotions, reflections, and lessons remain unfiltered and true. This is not anyone else's story, it is mine, shaped by memory, deepened by experience, and reframed through the lens of growth. I did not write these pages to expose another, I wrote them to reveal myself, to place my heart, at last, back into my own hands.

Life rarely unfolds in polished chapters. It circles in echoes, in patterns, in lessons that return until we dare to face them. These pages hold the moments when I began to see clearly. This book was born of truth, the kind that emerges only after you have loved deeply, been broken open, and chosen to rise again. If you find pieces of yourself reflected here, may it feel less like judgment and more like an invitation, an opening to pause, to reflect, to grow.

I wrote this book for women like us, women who have given and sacrificed, poured and prayed, only to discover that the love we nurtured was not the love we deserved. My story is not written to cast blame. It is written to name truth, to break silence, and to illuminate the places we too often keep hidden. At its heart, this memoir is about reclaiming my voice, honoring my resilience, and learning to choose myself, fully and without apology.

Each chapter does more than recount a story, it extends an invitation. Through spotlight reflections, unfiltered moments, and journal prompts, this book is designed not only to be read but to be experienced. Take your time. Sit with it. Write in the margins. Let your own story rise to meet mine.

Why me? Because, beyond being a woman who lived this, I bring nearly three decades of experience as a nurse, a caregiver, and a witness to resilience in its many forms. I know what it means to hold space for others, and what it costs when we forget to hold space for ourselves. As an entrepreneur, a mother, and a woman who has walked through grief, menopause, and rebirth, I write not from theory but from lived truth.

By the final page, I hope you leave with more than just my story. I hope you carry clarity about your own patterns, compassion for the woman you once were, and confidence in the woman you are becoming. May you learn to stop shrinking, to name your needs without shame, and to love yourself in ways that make room only for what aligns with your worth.

This is not merely my memoir. It is an invitation, an urging, for you to reclaim your story, your voice, and your truth. Thank you for walking with me. May these words give you permission to unmask your own truth, honor your echoes, and reclaim what has always belonged to you.

TABLE OF CONTENTS

***

PART I: THE MASK

I learned how easily charm can cover truth, and how costly it is to ignore my own reflection.

Chapter 1

THE SPARK THAT DIMMED MY LIGHT

"The spirit of man is the candle of the Lord." -- Proverbs 20:27 (KJV)

Long before I danced in a kitchen or whispered prayers with someone I hoped would stay, heartbreak showed me what it meant to dim. As a teenager, my first love ended abruptly. I loved unguarded and was unprepared for the break. I gave too much too soon. When he left me for someone else, I didn't just lose him, I lost my sense of worth.

"It's not you, it's just… I think I'm better with her," he told me back then, a blunt ending to a love I thought was forever.

I carried those words for years, always comparing myself to the girl he chose and measuring my worth against hers. That heartbreak was crushing.

That loss changed how I saw love. Instead of staying open, I sought out emotionally unavailable men, thinking that winning their affection proved my worth. I began to accept crumbs, mistaking routine for genuine care. Therapy helped me see this pattern. My adult love echoed my first heartbreak, believing that love meant proving myself to someone who was already looking elsewhere. Menopause clarified that. Sleepless nights exposed my ache, mood swings reduced my tolerance for half-love, and grief warned me not to keep losing myself.

So, when new sparks arrived, long talks, morning check-ins, prayers, and laughter in my kitchen, I allowed myself to believe this could finally be different.

In the beginning, everything flowed. We talked for hours about music, life, and dreams. There were morning check-ins, nightly prayers, and thoughtful messages.

"Good morning, just wanted to hear your voice before my day starts," he would say.

"Let's pray before bed, I want us covered," he would whisper over the phone.

The kitchen became our main stage. We could sit there for hours, voices spilling into the night, talking about everything. Sometimes the hum of the refrigerator was the only thing breaking the quiet between stories. Other nights, it was the living room, where the glow of the TV flickered across our faces as we stretched across the couch, binge-watching shows until we both drifted off. We would tickle each other until we were doubled over, gasping for air through the laughter, or play silly games that left us collapsing side by side, out of breath and still grinning.

Out in the world, we would lean against each other at a jazz lounge, whispering jokes in between sets, or sit on a park bench people-watching, making up elaborate backstories about strangers passing by. A woman in red heels became a runaway bride, and a man pacing on his phone became an undercover spy. Our laughter made the ordinary feel extraordinary.

Dates felt intentional, games, concerts, and late nights filled with music. Even after those outings, we would replay the funniest or craziest things we had seen, laughing again like we were reliving the night.

There were nights dancing in the kitchen while pasta boiled on the stove, garlic sizzled in the pan, and candles flickered low, Stevie Wonder, Michael Jackson, whoever was on the playlist. Sometimes the lyrics were off, and sometimes we twirled until the laughter was bigger than the song itself.

"You know you can't dance, right?" I would tease, spinning away from him.

"Maybe not, but you're smiling and that's all I need," he would reply, pulling me back.

Discovering how ticklish we both were became its own inside joke, me dodging his hands as I clutched a dish towel, him laughing when I would catch him off guard. The smell of garlic in the pan, mixed with the warm candlelight and our laughter, made the kitchen more than a place to cook, it was a stage for joy.

Those simple joys made me think, maybe this is it. I chose to hold onto those moments, even when flickers of distance quietly appeared alongside them.

I heard stories of past relationships framed in ways that cast the other person as unsupportive, with the storyteller positioned as misunderstood.

"She never had my back. Nobody ever really did," he would say, voice heavy with self-pity.

I listened, but a quiet voice inside reminded me that there is always more to a story.

When I voiced a different view, the temperature could drop, and conversation could give way to quiet. Later, there would be apologies, sweet gestures, and reassurances. "I just want us to be okay," he would murmur, handing me flowers.

I chalked it up to stress, but that was the first time I noticed myself begin to shrink.

Relationships moved quickly. I adjusted my schedule, traveled often, stayed for stretches, planned surprises, and mailed cards. I thought I was pouring into something mutual. But each time I returned home, I felt more drained.

Gestures sometimes arrived as financial help or shiny tokens, generous on the surface. But what I longed for was not a transaction. I wanted thoughtfulness, to be seen without having to say it. At the time, I tucked that longing away.

There were hints, subtle but steady, that if the relationship ever faltered, the blame would land at my feet.

"If this ever ends, it won't be because of me," he would declare, words I once mistook as reassurance.

At the time, I heard it as a vow to keep us together. Now I hear it differently, a warning wrapped in charm that shifted the weight of responsibility onto me before I even knew it.

So often, what I was really witnessing was searching, validation, comfort, a mirror to reflect worth back. I did not realize I was being asked to become that mirror.

And because a part of me, the little girl who longed to be chosen, wanted so badly to believe, I held onto the moments, the kitchen dancing, the music trivia, the sense that we were building something real.

It is easy to romanticize the spark when you have been waiting to feel its warmth again.

Spotlight Reflection

Love can feel like a full room and still leave you standing alone in the corner.

Unfiltered Moment

Sometimes the one who makes you feel most seen at first is the same one who disappears when you finally need to be held.

Journal Prompts

- What were the earliest signs that something did not feel right, even when it looked perfect?

- Where did you silence your intuition to hold onto a spark that was already fading?
- How has your earliest heartbreak, and the way you processed it, shaped what you accepted or pursued in adult love?

But that spark did not last. And in time, it dimmed me.

✍ Journal Here:

Chapter 2

ROUTINE AIN'T THE SAME AS REAL

"Let there be spaces in your togetherness." – Kahlil Gibran, The Prophet (1923)

There were days I would sit in silence after calls, asking myself: Am I too sensitive? Am I asking for too much? Deep down, I knew the truth. I was shrinking, bit by bit, to fit into someone else's version of love. And I promised myself that one day I would stop doing that.

Early on, when I felt the edges of communication beginning to fray, I suggested therapy. Not because anything was broken, but because I believed in growing with intention.

"What do you think about us trying therapy?" I asked one evening. "Not because something is wrong, because it could help us grow."

His response was quick, almost dismissive.

"Therapy? That's for married people, or couples already in trouble. We don't need that, we're fine."

The sharpness in his tone lingered. I had heard that same kind of reluctance before. Some dismissed therapy as playing house. Others believed that if two people could not work it out on their own, they did not belong together in the first place. Different words, same reluctance.

To me, therapy was not pretending, it was preparing. It was about building the foundation we kept talking about. Why wait to care for something we said we valued?

So, I went back to therapy on my own. Life had stacked loss on top of pressure. Over the years, I had carried the weight of losing people close to me, grief I had not fully dealt with. I was also carrying the emotional weight of starting over in business. I needed a place to process, to breathe, to be reminded that my needs were valid. Therapy became the one room where I did not have to shrink to fit.

One afternoon, Dr. Clark looked at me and asked:

"Tanya, you keep telling me what you did, how you showed up, planned, forgave, extended grace. But how did you feel in it?"

The question hit harder than I expected. I realized how often I explained his choices while glossing over my own feelings.

"I felt unseen," I admitted. "Like I could pour and pour, and it was never enough to fill him. I thought that if I adjusted, if I loved harder, the routine would turn into a real connection."

"And what did that cost you?" she pressed.

"My peace. My joy. Pieces of myself."

She nodded gently, then leaned in. "Tanya, grief isn't linear. It's okay to not be okay. Be gentle with yourself. Why do you feel the need to explain so much?"

I swallowed. The answer sat heavily. "Because if I could explain it well enough, maybe he would finally see me. Maybe he would care differently."

Dr. Clark shook her head. "His actions had nothing to do with you and everything to do with him. What you were missing in the relationship, what you didn't speak on, mattered. Don't ignore that."

Her words became both a mirror and a balm. She asked me to hold up the small mirror she kept on her desk. "Why did you allow yourself to shrink?" she asked softly. I stared at my reflection, uncomfortable but unwilling to look away.

She leaned in gently. "Routine without reciprocity isn't love, it is convenience. Be careful not to confuse consistency with intimacy."

When things were good, they were good. Sunday mornings wrapped in warmth, concerts under the stars, long belly laughs, and slow dances that lingered. We would stretch out on the couch, legs tangled, binge-watching shows until empty snack bowls sat on the table between us. The steady glow of a candle lit nearby gave the room a comfort I did not realize I craved. Other nights, we sat cross-legged on the floor, swapping childhood stories, voices dropping low when we confessed the harder parts.

At concerts, I leaned into his shoulder under the night sky, the bass rattling in my chest while his hand rested steady on mine. Even in public, we found joy in people-watching, whispering back-and-forth commentary, inventing stories about strangers like two kids daring each other to imagine wilder tales. Those moments built a world that felt like it belonged only to us.

Those good moments had weight, but so did the empty spaces. And eventually, the silence grew louder than the sweet gestures.

Because routine is not the same as real. At first, the predictability felt like safety, the good morning calls, the late-night prayers, even his habit of sending me the same song for days in a row. It was comforting, until it became choreography without heart.

There was consistency, but not curiosity. Access, but not intimacy. I could be welcomed yet not fully seen. Wanted, but not always valued.

I noticed the small things first. Belongings were moved and not returned. Choices made together were suddenly replaced without conversation. When I asked gently if something felt off, the answer was predictable: "You're reading too much into it."

But I wasn't. I was listening to the pauses, the omissions, the quiet shifts that said more than words ever did.

Dr. Clark asked me to write down what being a priority meant. That night, I journaled: feeling valued, respected, and seen. Quality time without prompting. Boundaries honored. Conflict handled with care.

When I read it aloud to her, my voice trembled. They weren't demands. They were the bare minimum.

I didn't need perfection. I needed presence. Someone who didn't have to be prompted to care. A love that could sit in discomfort and say, "We will figure this out, together."

Instead, I was often met with logic, with deflection, with silence.

I offered tools. I extended grace. I reached for the "we" that was always spoken of. But growth kept getting delayed, postponed until some undefined future milestone.

Eventually, I got honest with myself.

Love, to me, looks like partnership, not performance. It looks like repair, not routine. It looks like being seen, not just scheduled in.

I kept showing up. I kept trying. Until I realized I didn't need to prove I belonged. I just needed to believe I did, and act like it.

I had known this rhythm before. Relationships where presence looked predictable but felt hollow. Where I was penciled in but not prioritized. Where gestures were repeated like choreography, neat, polished, even reliable, but never reaching into the deeper places of who I was. The common thread was always the same: routine mistaken for intimacy, performance mistaken for care.

And because I had learned long ago to accept partial love as better than none, I lingered.

Dr. Clark didn't let me linger in denial. She reminded me:

"Routine without reciprocity isn't love, it's convenience. And Tanya, you deserve more than convenience."

Grief showed up here, too, not only grief for people I had lost, but grief for parts of myself I had abandoned in exchange for staying chosen.

Perimenopause only heightened the ache. Nights of broken sleep left me thinner in patience. Hot flashes in the middle of conversations made me wish for tenderness instead of teasing.

"You're burning up again? That's crazy," he would laugh, when what I longed for was compassion.

Brain fog stole words from my mouth, and instead of leaning closer, I often felt partners lean away, choosing distraction over presence. My body's changes forced me to confront the difference between stability and safety.

What I longed for was refuge, a love that could sit with the ordinary, the tired, the unfiltered, and still call it enough.

Spotlight Reflection

When care is real, it survives the ordinary. If someone can show up for the event but not for the everyday, you don't have a partner, you have a pattern.

Unfiltered Moment

Consistency without curiosity is just choreography. I don't want rehearsed love; I want present love.

Therapist's Notes: What I Learned About Relationships

- Lack of effective communication erodes trust.
- Holding on to unresolved issues turns love into landmines.
- Boundaries matter, and so does honoring them.
- Both partners must be healed and self-aware before stepping into a relationship.
- Some relationships exist to serve a purpose, not a lifetime.

Journal Prompts

- Where have I confused routine for a real connection?
- What reassurances do I need to feel emotionally safe, and have I named them out loud?
- Which subtle shifts, the tiny omissions and "forgot" gestures, have I explained away? What happens if I take them at face value?
- How have my body's changes, including fatigue, mood shifts, and sleepless nights, shaped what I need most from love right now?

Conditional care doesn't just limit love, it distorts reality. Soon, what I needed turned into debates about what was true.

✍ Journal Here:

Chapter 3

WHEN CARE WAS CONDITIONAL

"Perfect love casteth out fear." – 1 John 4:18 (KJV)

e used to talk about support as if it were a shared language.

"Tell me what you need," he'd say.

So, I did.

I told him plainly: support, to me, looked like presence, not gifts, not sweet words. It looked like showing up to the things that mattered to me, stepping into my world the same way I stepped into his.

And the answer always sounded easy:

"Say less. I got you."

But care that has to be begged for isn't care. Promises without follow-through fade like smoke.

I invited openly, early, and often.

"If you can come, I'd love to see you there."

Warm reassurances followed. But when the day came, there was always a shift: a last-minute text, a sudden excuse, a gentle "next time." And even on the occasions he did show up, the presence wasn't whole, his body in the room, his spirit elsewhere.

Still, the good memories softened the truth. Curled up on the couch, laughing at a show we promised to binge. Teasing each other until we were breathless from tickle fights. Quiet hours in the kitchen, trading stories about our pasts. Even people-watching in a café, inventing strangers' life stories together. Those moments felt like intimacy stitched in laughter, and they convinced me to wait for the "next time" that rarely came.

I tried naming it without blame.

"Support isn't a checklist," I explained. "It's about choosing to care in my language, not just yours."

He nodded, but his actions never shifted. What I needed, versus what he decided was enough, never met in the middle. Support arrived on his terms, at his convenience, on his timeline.

The smaller tells cut deepest. Wins in my work were brushed aside with a quick, "That's nice, anyway…" My joy was forced to shrink while his needs filled the space. Even conversations about growth met resistance.

When I suggested therapy, not as a last resort but as an intentional step, he dismissed it.

"That's playing house," or "If two people can't work things out on their own, they don't belong together."

Different words. Same refusal.

Later, therapy gave me language for what I had felt. My need for deeper care was never unnecessary, it was essential.

Dr. Clark once leaned forward and asked, "What do you feel you were missing that you didn't speak on?"

I hesitated. "Consistency. Emotional safety. Someone who could sit with me in silence without making me feel like I was asking too much."

She held up a mirror. "Look at yourself. Why did you allow yourself to shrink?"

The question gutted me.

"Because I thought love required it," I whispered. "If I made myself smaller, easier, more accommodating, it would keep the peace. It would keep me chosen."

But shrinking didn't save me. It erased me.

And still, truth slipped through his guard. Admissions surfaced, acknowledgment that what I asked for was simple. That I had shown up, and his pride stood in the way. Hearing it confirmed I hadn't imagined our conversations. My needs were understood, admitted as worthy, and still not chosen.

I had asked for flowers. But it was never about flowers. It was about proving that I mattered: effort, presence, follow-through.

He once admitted it aloud. "All she wanted was flowers." Then, almost proudly, he added, "I was too ornery to do it."

Another time, under a haze of pride and performance, he said, "She just simply wants to be your wife."

That sentence lodged in my chest. Proof that he heard me, understood me, and still refused to move. It wasn't confusion, it was a refusal.

The cruelty wasn't in the absence of gestures. It was in the awareness. He knew, and he chose not to.

Over time, my needs weren't just dismissed. They were diminished. If I asked for closeness, I was "doing too much." If I asked for clarity, I was "making it a thing." And when I stopped reminding, stopped inviting, I saw how quickly the connection withered.

It couldn't breathe without my effort.

And all of this collided with the season my body was in.

Perimenopause was a demanding presence: fatigue begging for gentleness, restlessness for patience, change for companionship. I needed care that showed up in action, not excuses. Yet too often, I was met with dismissal instead of comfort.

Here's what I know now:

1. Care doesn't make you audition.
2. Care doesn't punish you for needing.
3. Care doesn't turn presence into a debate.

I kept showing up because that's my nature. He kept choosing comfort because that was his.

And eventually, I had to say it out loud:

If love needs me to shrink in order to survive, it isn't love. It's access, proximity dressed up as a partnership, care with conditions.

Spotlight Reflection

Support isn't a speech, it's a pattern. If you have to explain the same need more than once, you're not asking for too much, you're asking the wrong person.

Unfiltered Moment

I don't need perfect effort. I need honest effort, without being made to feel like the cost of it.

Journal Prompts

- Where have you accepted "next time" as a substitute for presence?
- When you define support in your own words, what does it look and feel like?
- What would you stop doing today if you believed your needs didn't make you "too much"?

- How does your body remind you when care is absent, even before your mind admits it?

Naming the conditions of love was only the beginning. The harder truth came next: seeing how quickly those conditions turned into cycles of blame and gaslighting, I could no longer ignore.

✍ Journal Here:

Chapter 4

BLAME, GASLIGHT, REPEAT

"If you tell the truth, you don't have to remember anything." – Mark Twain

There's a specific type of exhaustion that comes from constantly questioning yourself, not because you're unsure, but because someone keeps convincing you that your reality is flawed.

At first, I thought they were simple misunderstandings. Two grown adults, just wired differently, right? But over time, those "misunderstandings" revealed a pattern: blame-shifting and gaslighting.

It could be as small as a misplaced remote.

"You must have moved it. I can never find things after you've been in here," he said.
"I haven't touched it," I'd reply, steady but stung.
"Every time, it's always you."

I'd scan the room, the hum of the TV in the background, the faint smell of last night's takeout still in the air. Hours later, the remote would turn up right where he had left it. No apology, just a flat, "I found it."

And then, as if the sting didn't matter, he'd change the subject.

The damage wasn't in being wrong, it was in the reflex to assign blame before seeking truth. That reflex taught me my voice wasn't the first one trusted, even when the evidence was plain.

It wasn't isolated. These were the steady drips of small cuts, bruising the inside while leaving no mark on the outside.

It showed up in other ways, too. Plans shifted, schedules changed, and instead of a conversation, I'd be met with sharpness.
"I never know what side of the bed you woke up on," he'd mutter when I asked why things had suddenly changed.
Anger where calm would have sufficed. Defensiveness where teamwork was needed. Always quick to explain, slow to listen.

Then came the distortions. My devotion recast as neglect.

"You always put your business and your people before me," he claimed one night, arms crossed, voice low.

I blinked, stunned. The lamp cast a soft glow on the table where I had spread out notes for his birthday surprise dinner. I had flown out to see him, rearranged my schedule, mailed cards, and carved time where none existed. And still, he rewrote my devotion as absence.

"Do you really believe that?" I asked, my voice catching.

He shrugged, eyes hard.

"I'm not a priority. That's just the truth."

His truth became the truth, while mine was dismissed as an overreaction. Love I gave freely was twisted into proof that I didn't give enough. That wasn't love, it was control disguised as expectation.

Sometimes, after I named something that hurt me, his response came cloaked in false nobility:

"I don't bring up everything that bothers me about you, because I know people aren't perfect. Stop being so hard on me."

It sounded gracious, but it wasn't. It was a warning: I'm keeping a list. Don't push me.

And it left me questioning. If there were things about me that bothered him, why not say them aloud? His silence didn't feel like grace. It felt like ammunition being stockpiled.

He often leaned on identity instead of accountability. After sharp words or careless actions that left me stung, the response was never, "I didn't mean to hurt you. I'm sorry." Instead, it was, "If you knew me, you'd know that's not my heart. That's not who I am."

It sounded almost noble, but it was really a deflection. The problem became not the harm he caused, but my supposed failure to "know him" deeply enough. My feelings were left unacknowledged, brushed aside under the banner of who he believed himself to be.

But intention doesn't erase impact. Whether it was in his "heart" or not, the pain landed in mine. My needs didn't require declarations of character; they required care, presence, and accountability.

And silence isn't grace. Silence is erasure. And I wasn't willing to erase myself, not in love and not in the middle of my own changes.

The kitchen smelled of garlic one evening, sauce simmering on the stove, when I tried to explain how dismissed I felt. His answer wasn't soft and wasn't apologetic.

"You're too emotional lately. Everything can't be about you."

The words cut through the warmth of the meal I was cooking. My body was already screaming for gentleness, perimenopause demanding rest, patience, and presence. But instead of comfort, I got criticism.

And when I called out selfishness, the script flipped.

"So now I'm selfish? That's what you think of me?"

When I sought honesty, the spotlight turned back on me.

"You're twisting this. I guess I can't do nothing right."

The contradictions were sharp and relentless. Conversations about growth never moved forward. Suggestions like therapy were revisited and waved away.

"We don't need that. We can handle this ourselves."

But what he meant was, I won't sit in a room where the truth can't be controlled.

Weeks later, I found myself sitting across from Dr. Clark, the soft tick of her clock filling the quiet between us. Therapy had become my space to untangle the knots I couldn't undo inside the relationship.

Dr. Clark leaned back in her chair, pen poised but eyes steady on me. "You've mentioned resistance a lot. Let's name it. What did his resistance feel like to you?"

I exhaled slowly. "Like a wall. Every time I tried to bring something up therapy, accountability, even just asking for presence, it was brick after brick. And I started to wonder if I was asking for too much."

She tilted her head. "Was it too much?"

"No." My voice was firmer than I expected. "It wasn't. It was honesty. It was care. It was the bare minimum."

She tapped her pen lightly against her notebook. "So why did it feel too much?"

"Because he made it feel that way. The resistance wasn't about me. It was about him, about fear. Fear of what the truth would require if he admitted it out loud."

Dr. Clark nodded. "Exactly. Resistance is rarely about the request. It's about the change the request demands. And if he could convince you that you were asking for too much, then he never had to face that change."

Her words landed like a key sliding into a lock.

I whispered, "That's the subtlety of manipulation. It hides in the gap between love and logic. It sounds like concern, looks like consistency, but it moves like control."

She let the silence hang, then asked, "So what did you learn from that pattern?"

I sat taller, the words rising in me like a vow.

"If I had to shrink to be heard, it wasn't listening.

If my needs had to be minimized to keep the peace, it wasn't peace. If my reality had to be rewritten to keep someone else comfortable, it wasn't love."

Dr. Clark smiled gently, her pen finally still. "That's not just a lesson, Tanya. That's your truth. Hold onto it."

Naming a pattern became more dangerous than enduring it. That's the dangerous subtlety of manipulation: it hides in the gap between love and logic. It sounds like concern, looks like consistency, but moves like control.

Here's what I had to learn:

1. If I had to shrink to be heard, it wasn't listening.
2. If my needs had to be minimized to keep the peace, it wasn't peace.
3. If my reality had to be rewritten to keep someone else comfortable, it wasn't love.

Eventually, I stopped shrinking.
Eventually, I chose truth.
Even when it hurt.
Even when it meant seeing the pattern clearly and letting go of the version I wanted to believe in.

Spotlight Reflection

Gaslighting often starts as "helpful correction." Notice who blames first and asks questions later.

Unfiltered Moment

I can hold grace and still hold a boundary. Your comfort doesn't get to cost me my clarity.

Journal Prompts

- Recall a time you were blamed before anyone looked for facts. What did that teach you about safety with that person?
- Where have you labeled your silence as "grace"? What would honest grace, with truth, look like instead?
- When you name a pattern, does your partner get curious or defensive? What does that tell you?

- How did exhaustion, grief, or hormonal shifts shape the way you heard criticism, and what kind of care would have felt different?

Blame and distortion left me weary, but what came next showed me how quickly weariness can turn into wake-up calls.

✍ Journal Here:

Chapter 5

I WAS THERE. HE WASN'T.

"Consistency is a love language, absence is an answer." – Tanya T. Bennett

I don't know how they couldn't see it.

I showed up in every way that mattered physically, emotionally, logistically, spiritually. I didn't wait to be asked; I just moved, rearranged my schedule, set work aside, and made it happen so we could build something that felt real. I was consistent, present, intentional.

Birthdays and holidays? I didn't just celebrate, I honored. I planned moments that mattered, weaving in details that spoke directly to who they were and what they loved. I made sure no one important was left out, even creating ways for those far away to be included. It wasn't performative, it was purposeful. That's how I love: with detail and intention.

The contrast was sharp on my own birthdays. Time for me was often squeezed in, as if celebrating me was something to fit into the day rather than the day being about me. The default became: Treat yourself, pick an outfit, get your nails done. I'll cover it. Generous? Maybe. Thoughtful? Not quite. That was funding, not forethought, something anybody with a card could do. What I craved didn't cost much: a morning at the museum, lakeside walks, ballet tickets, and flowers because he knew I loved them. But I rarely received the kind of surprise that whispered, I see you.

I wanted presence without prompting. I wanted the details I had already spoken aloud to be remembered. I wanted support to look like showing up, not being reminded to.

There were weekends I stepped away from responsibilities, moments that mattered to me, just so I could keep plans. I even adjusted trips and shifted my own commitments to be available when asked. At the time, I called it a partnership, flexibility, what love does.

What I needed in return was simple: someone to notice the weight I was carrying as an entrepreneur, to cheer me on, to hold space for the fear that crept in some nights, to celebrate the little wins. But too often, when I invited others into that space, they stood on the sidelines physically present but emotionally checked out.

I remember one evening when he FaceTimed me after receiving a call from his sister. The concern on his face told the story before he even spoke.

"My niece is in the hospital," he said. "But she didn't say I needed to come home. I'll wait for more information."

I shook my head gently. "Sometimes the strong ones don't ask. She's probably been carrying it on her own for so long that asking doesn't even feel like an option. But that doesn't mean she doesn't need you."

He looked torn. "But she didn't say it."

"You don't need to wait for her to spell it out," I told him. "Your niece needs to know you care enough to just show up. And your sister will feel that in ways she can't put into words. Let me pick you up from the airport."

A few days later, I did just that. When he walked into that hospital room, his sister's eyes filled with gratitude, and his niece cried tears that needed no explanation. Later, he admitted, "I'm glad I came. I didn't know how much I needed to be here until I was."

The irony came later, when I showed up for him and was met not with gratitude but resentment.

And in the middle of all that absence, I'll never forget the day I came home, exchanged a few words with my dad, and headed back out. As I walked toward the door, he looked at me and said quietly, "Tell him I said to send you home."

I paused for a moment, then said, "I'll be back soon, Dad." But he repeated himself: "Tell him what I said."

I thought it strange for Daddy to say that, and I shrugged it off. I never did tell him what Daddy said. And now I wonder what would have been the result if I had? Why, after all that time, did he choose those words?

Not long after, Daddy was gone. His words remain a mystery, unfinished, like a warning left hanging in the air.

And then there was my mother. She admitted to me later that she had prayed for God to remove him from my life. She saw hurt written in the way things were unfolding, and she didn't want me to be the one left carrying it. A mother's prayer is never small. To hear that she spoke to God on my behalf, asking Him to protect me from the very love I thought I needed, cut deep but it also revealed how much she was watching and how much she cared.

My father's warning and my mother's prayer weren't just passing moments. They were mirrors, reflecting what I refused to see: that I was giving my all to something that only gave back in fragments. I convinced myself it was love, but they knew better. They saw the imbalance, the exhaustion, the quiet breaking of my spirit.

It wasn't until therapy that I could finally name it.

Dr. Clark sat across from me as I shared the story of my father's words. "Tell him I said to send you home," I repeated aloud. The sentence still hung heavy.

She leaned forward. "What do you think he was seeing that you couldn't?"

I swallowed. "That I was fading, that I was pouring out everything and receiving scraps in return. He saw the imbalance before I admitted it to myself."

"And your mother's prayer?" she asked gently.

I blinked back tears. "That one broke me. Because it meant she knew. She was watching me love myself into exhaustion, and she begged God to intervene."

Dr. Clark let the silence hold for a moment, then said, "Sometimes those who love us most have the clearest vision. They see what we normalize."

I nodded, my voice low. "I thought I was being loyal. But what I was really doing was betraying myself."

She tapped her pen lightly. "And now?"

"Now I can say it plainly. I was there. Present. Whole. He wasn't."

Her eyes softened. "Say that again."

I inhaled deeply, exhaled slowly. "I was there. He wasn't."

Dr. Clark nodded, then asked, "And what does that truth mean for you going forward?"

I felt my throat tighten, but the words rose anyway.

"Here's the truth: you don't have to beg someone to see you when their eyes are open but their heart is closed. Presence isn't complicated. Love doesn't need reminders. If it's real, it shows up."

Dr. Clark smiled, the kind of smile that carried both affirmation and release. "That's not just healing, Tanya. That's freedom."

Spotlight Reflection

What you repeat reveals what you value. When love is present, presence is, too. Me

Unfiltered Moment

I kept curating moments that said "us" while accepting patterns that said "me," alone. The day I stopped confusing generosity with intimacy, I stopped negotiating my worth. — Me

Journal Prompts

- Where have you been funding connection instead of cultivating intimacy?
- What does "showing up" look like in your language of love, and how will you state that clearly?
- Which small, consistent behaviors make you feel safe and seen, and how will you require them without apology?
- How does your body respond when presence is missing, and what practices bring you back to yourself?

✍ Journal Here:

____

____

____

____

____

____

____

CHAPTER ECHO: CLOSING PART I – THE MASK

- I was there in full color.
- They showed up in outline.
- The mask I wore wasn't just theirs, it was mine, too.
- And lifting it was the first step toward reclaiming me.

PART II: THE UNSEEN & UNSAID

Every silence I kept became a weight I carried, until I could no longer deny the toll of my own sacrifices.

Chapter 6

INVISIBLE SACRIFICES

"Thy Father which seeth in secret himself shall reward thee openly." — Matthew 6:4 (KJV)

Some kinds of love aren't loud. They don't sparkle on timelines or beg for applause. They show up in silence, in the margins. A warm hand on a cold day. A stocked shelf. A whispered prayer no one hears but God.

I learned to love quietly, to be present without fanfare. I paid attention to what made life easier and folded those details into my days: favorite snacks refilled, blankets washed just right, text messages sent before the hours that always seemed the hardest. Not for recognition, just to say, I see you.

I cooked meals I knew would be missed otherwise. I nudged about appointments and checked in afterward, not because I wanted a gold star, but because I wanted the people I loved to be well. When life made us ships passing, I bent my calendar so we could anchor at the same time, even if that anchoring happened on a screen.

There is a deep precision in quiet love. It's not meek. It's mindful. And I didn't just do the soft work of love, I did the work on the relationship. Early on, I invested in tools for growth: books about love languages, guides for building connection, resources for deeper dialogue. Too often, they sat unopened. Later, in therapy, I gathered more tools: scripts to spark honest conversations, frameworks for the heart-to-hearts we promised to have the next time we were in the same space. But the tools remained untouched, the conversations postponed, the growth delayed.

So, I opened my schedule instead. Rearranged calls. Pushed deadlines back. So I could be there, for us.

What did that cost? More than time. More than sleep. It cost pieces of me I didn't realize I was giving away.

There's a difference between being low-maintenance and being low-priority. I wasn't asking for grand gestures. I just wanted to be met with the same intentionality I was giving. I showed up with thoughtfulness and care. Too often, what came back was convenience and assumption.

Some of those sacrifices, if I'm honest, didn't even start from love. They started from fear, from the part of me still hoping to be chosen. I thought that if I stayed soft enough, quiet enough, helpful enough, no one would leave. I don't resent her. She kept me safe for a long time. But safety and wholeness are not the same thing. Therapy later showed me the grief hidden inside that pattern, because every time I made myself invisible to hold onto love, I lost another piece of me.

When love is mutual, quiet care feels sacred. When it's one-sided, it becomes a form of erasure.

I carried weight I didn't create. Partners hadn't healed from wounds that came before me, and somewhere along the line, I became the placeholder for her.

Her mistakes. Her betrayals. Her echoes. It was never said outright, but I felt it: the suspicion in the silence, the guardedness behind affection, the way walls didn't lower no matter how gently I knocked. I was paying for damage I didn't do. I kept hoping that if I just loved better, deeper, more patiently, I could prove I wasn't her.

I wasn't her. I didn't break them. I didn't create the wound. I just bled from it. That's the cost of invisible care: when your love becomes a salve for someone else's scars, but you're still blamed when it stings.

That's what I told Dr. Clark one afternoon, eyes fixed on the floor between us.

She let the silence stretch, then asked, "What did it feel like to pay for someone else's mistakes?"

"Exhausting," I whispered. "Like bleeding for a crime I didn't commit."

"And why did you agree to pay that price?"

My throat tightened. "Because I thought if I gave enough, he'd stop seeing me through her shadow. That eventually, I'd be different enough, good enough, consistent enough to erase what she did."

Dr. Clark leaned forward, her voice gentle but firm. "Tanya, love doesn't require you to compete with ghosts. That wasn't your healing to carry."

Her words cracked something in me. For the first time, I saw it not as loyalty but as labor I was never meant to perform.

There was one moment that changed everything. A sabbatical had been gifted to me, a solo retreat to rest, reset, and breathe. I shared it, excited. His response was to attach: "I'll come too."

I said no. Kindly. Clearly. This was given to me, for me. The reaction wasn't loud, but the silence carried a price tag: "Go, and see what happens when you get back." That's when I saw it clearly: not love, but control dressed as closeness. Not protection, but possession.

Still, I packed my bag, sweats, sneakers, a journal, and a promise I made to myself before anyone else had a vote: I am allowed to be well. And I went.

When I came back, Dr. Clark asked, "What did you notice most while you were away?"

"That my body exhaled in ways it hadn't in years," I said. "The silence didn't scare me. It healed me."

"And what truth does that tell you?" she pressed.

"That love isn't supposed to feel like erasure. That is when I stop performing, I should still be safe. And if I'm only valued for what I sacrifice, then I was never truly seen."

She nodded. "That's the cost of invisible sacrifices: you become invisible, too. And Tanya, you were never meant to disappear."

That week, I remembered what it felt like to breathe without performance. I woke up without panic. Ate when I was hungry, rested when I was tired. I listened to God in the stillness, not through someone else's chaos. And I cried, not because I was heartbroken, but because my nervous system finally had space to tell the truth.

That trip didn't end the relationship, but it ended the part of me that thought I needed permission to care for myself. When I came back, I carried a different kind of clarity: not the kind that screams, but the kind that rearranges everything so the doorway to yourself is no longer blocked.

Perimenopause turned invisible sacrifice into something I could feel under my skin. It wasn't just emotional, it was physical. The more I set myself aside, the more my body responded with restlessness, fatigue, and an ache I couldn't stretch away. What I carried quietly began showing up loudly in my health, my patience, and my peace.

Spotlight Reflection

If the only evidence of love is your labor, you haven't built intimacy. You've built infrastructure.

Unfiltered Moment

What I gave in silence, my body told the truth about: fatigue, restlessness, the ache of being unseen. Love isn't supposed to feel like fading.

Journal Prompts

- Where did I call a sacrifice "love" when it was really self-abandonment?
- Which boundaries felt negotiable then but are non-negotiable now?

- What spiritual, physical, or creative rituals did I put down to "keep the peace," and which will I pick up first?
- How will I tell the difference between compromise and erasure in my next season?

Quiet self-erasure has a cousin: the steady forgetting of your own needs. Naming mine became the next threshold.

✍ Journal Here:

Chapter 7

THE FRACTURE THAT STAYED

"What you allow is what will continue." — Author Unknown

There are moments that don't break you all at once but leave a crack you can never quite seal. That day, I didn't bounce back. Something stayed lodged in my spirit, no matter how much I tried to move forward.

It started over something small. The kind of moment most couples would have talked through and moved past. Earlier that day, he had spoken to me sharply, dismissively, in a tone that caught me off guard. It wasn't what he said as much as *how* he said it. Clipped, impatient, as if my question had already annoyed him before I finished asking it.

I let it pass at first. I often did.
Not because it didn't matter, but because I knew how quickly bringing things up could shift the atmosphere.

But as the day went on, the words stayed with me. The tone lingered. And by the time we were alone again, I realized what I needed wasn't an argument — it was acknowledgment. I wasn't looking to revisit the moment to assign blame. I just wanted to name how it landed.

That's when I decided to say something.

I had already learned how to enter conversations with him carefully.
Not honestly—carefully.

I wasn't preparing to argue. I was preparing to manage the moment.
Tone first. Timing second. Truth last.

I remember standing there, aware of how my body felt before a single word landed—shoulders tight, chest shallow, breath measured. I knew what this conversation *could* turn into if I wasn't precise.

"Can I say something?" I asked, already softening my voice.

He sighed—not loud, but heavy enough to let me know I was already on thin ice.

"What now?" he said.

"I just want to talk about how that came across earlier," I said. "It didn't sit right with me."

His tone shifted immediately.

"Here we go," he muttered. "You always do this."

I paused—not because I didn't know what to say, but because I knew how quickly the wrong sentence could escalate things.

"I'm not trying to start anything," I said, slower now. "I'm saying I didn't like how you spoke to me."

He laughed—not amused, not kind.

"See, that's what I'm talking about," he snapped. "Everything turns into a problem with you."

I felt myself shrinking in real time.

I replied. "I'm just letting you know how that made me feel."

"Oh, I guess I just can't do nothing right," he cut in. "I can't say nothing without you taking it the wrong way."

That was the moment I realized I wasn't being heard—I was being tolerated.

I stopped mid-thought, weighing whether continuing was worth it. I adjusted my words again, gentler this time, even though nothing about the way he was speaking to me felt gentle.

"That's not what I said," I replied.

"I don't have the energy for this," he said sharply. "I don't have to put up with this."

The disagreement had spun out of control, accusations that didn't make sense, words sharper than truth, and a charge that I was being disrespectful simply because I walked around the house in silence. What he didn't understand was that silence wasn't distance. It was care. It was me trying to shape my words so they could be received without confusion, without explosion.

But he ran with his version of the story. And then, for a moment, he ran from me. He said he didn't want it anymore. Those words hung heavy in the room, sharp and final. Even though my heart whispered that wasn't what I wanted, I let him have his choice. I made it clear it wasn't mine, but I would never beg someone to stay. I respected the decision, even if I didn't agree with it.

Hours passed in silence. The weight of it pressed down on me like a stone. My chest rose and fell, but nothing about that silence felt like peace. It was suffocating, not soothing. And then, just as quickly as he had withdrawn, he shifted.

"This isn't worth throwing away," he said, his tone suddenly softer.

I remember looking at him, my head tilted, my heart racing with confusion. "What changed?" I asked out loud, desperate for something clear, something real. But he could never explain. Not then, not ever. In the absence of clarity, the strength I'd been holding onto finally gave way. The words came out smaller than I intended. His voice softened, almost curious.

"What's wrong with you?" he asked.

I opened my mouth to speak, but nothing clear came out. The ache behind my eyes spread to my chest, and before I could form a sentence, tears blurred my vision.

"I don't know," I whispered, shaking my head. "I don't know what's wrong with me. I just know I need help, and I don't even know how to tell you how to help me."

He stared for a moment, then reached for me, his hand tentative, almost careful. For a second, I let myself believe it meant he saw me, that maybe, finally, he understood the weight I was carrying.

But the touch stopped at the surface. No words. No follow-through. No effort to meet what I was trying to name. The quiet between us returned, pressing against my ribs until it ached.

I wasn't looking for him to fix me. I was asking to be felt, to be seen without having to explain the ache. But instead, his silence filled the space where comfort should have been.

In that stillness, I realized something I'd been avoiding for far too long: love without understanding isn't safety, it's solitude dressed in companionship. And I was tired of feeling alone next to someone who said he loved me.

A few days later, we circled back to the argument. I told him plainly how I felt and that the way he had spoken to me would never happen again. I don't care how angry a person is, what circumstances brought them to that anger, or what an ex may have done that triggered them, there is never an excuse to speak to me with disrespect or to speak down to me. I've always had that standard, and I hold it firmly. That day, I made sure he understood that boundary.

Even with that boundary set, something in me didn't recover. I tried. I told myself to move on, to let it go, to smooth it over. But every disagreement after that carried me back to that wound. Every explosion of emotion, every sharp response, felt like déjà vu. The details changed, but the fracture stayed the same.

It was as if the argument had carved a groove in my spirit, and no matter how much I wanted to climb out of it, every new moment of conflict slid me right back down. The wound wasn't just about what was said that day, it was about the rupture of trust, the shattering of safety, the knowing that he could so easily decide we weren't worth it, only to backpedal without reason. That kind of instability doesn't fade. It lingers. It grows louder in the quiet.

I carried that heaviness into therapy with Dr. Clark. I told her about the accusations, the silence, the sudden reversal from "I don't want this" to "This isn't worth throwing away." My words tumbled out in pieces, a mixture of anger, sadness, and confusion.

She listened, then asked softly, "Tanya, what did you need in that moment that you didn't get?"

The question hit me like a stone dropped into still water. I swallowed hard. "Safety. Understanding. Space to be heard without being accused."

She leaned in. "And what did you get instead?"

"Confusion," I whispered. "Distance. Explosions."

Dr. Clark nodded slowly, her gaze steady on mine. "That's why your spirit never bounced back. You were still waiting for a need to be met that he had already decided he wouldn't honor."

Her words wrapped around me like both a balm and a blade. A balm because they named what I couldn't, a blade because they sliced through the denial I had been carrying. The fracture wasn't just in the moment; it was in the absence of repair afterward. That's what lived in me. That's what replayed every time silence turned sharp again.

I wanted so badly to believe that we could press past it, that love could smooth over the fracture. But the truth is, I carried that break with me into every silence, every disagreement, every uneasy moment after. I was still present, still loving, still trying, but something in me had already begun to let go.

Spotlight Reflection

Some wounds don't announce themselves with screams or scars. They whisper in your spirit, reminding you every time a new hurt brushes against the old one. This wasn't just about words spoken in anger; it was about what stayed with me afterward. When your peace keeps tugging at you, it's not a betrayal of love. It's truth asking to be heard.

Unfiltered Moment

The boundary was clear. The line was drawn. And yet, even with words spoken and standards held, the wound stayed open. Respect is nonnegotiable, but repair is essential, and without it, fractures become fault lines that keep splitting wider.

Journal Prompts

- When have I felt something in my spirit shift and never fully return to its original place?
- How do I usually respond when I feel a crack in a relationship? Do I patch it, ignore it, or honor it?
- What boundaries have I set that were born from a moment I could not bounce back from?
- How can I learn to trust those quiet whispers in my spirit sooner, before they turn into loud lessons?

Carrying that fracture forward meant living with a steady ache, one that only grew louder as my needs continued to be overlooked. The question pressed in on me more and more: where were my needs in all of this?

✍ Journal Here:

____

____

____

____

____

____

Chapter 8

WHERE WERE MY NEEDS?

"When you spend all your energy meeting everyone else's needs, your own go unheard until the silence becomes unbearable." – Tanya T. Bennett

There was another truth I carried quietly, one I never fully said out loud: he stopped reaching for me, not just emotionally, but physically.

In the beginning, I named what I loved, plain and simple. Fresh flowers on ordinary days. A ticket to the ballet. A slow walk by the lake. Small gestures that felt like intention, not obligation.

Some of those things showed up early on, just enough to keep hope alive. But over time, joy turned into reminders, then disappointments, then arguments that left me feeling like I was begging to be considered in my own relationship. Partners loved to say they were "great daters," and yes, plans were made, but often around what already mattered to them: sporting events, concerts, familiar spots where they shined. These were fine joys, but as months passed, it became clear: they didn't want a partnership. They wanted an audience.

I knew how to show up for everyone else, for family, for friends, for love. It was my default setting: step in, give, hold space, keep things together. But the quiet question I avoided for too long was this: who was showing up for me?

There was a time when he would pull me close without hesitation, kiss me like he meant it, and touch me like he truly saw me. But slowly, almost silently, that changed. The compliments faded. The desire thinned. Days slipped into weeks without him telling me I was beautiful, without him reaching for me in a way that made me feel wanted, chosen, or desired.

I stopped feeling sexy around him. I stopped feeling seen as a woman, not in the ways that matter behind closed doors, and not in the intimate spaces where love is supposed to reassure you. I felt myself shrinking into the background of a relationship I was still trying to nurture, wondering which part of me had become invisible.

It wasn't just the absence of sex.

It was the absence of being wanted.

And that is a kind of loneliness that settles deep in the bones.

There was another moment I didn't name right away, one that quietly shifted how I began to experience myself in the relationship. It came during a conversation about the future, the kind that brushes up against commitment without ever resting there.

Marriage was spoken of as a possibility, framed in hypotheticals rather than intention. And almost seamlessly, the focus turned elsewhere.

Instead of talking about what building together might look like, the conversation moved toward evaluation. Questions followed. Curiosity that didn't feel mutual. Attention on my financial life, introduced without the grounding of commitment or shared responsibility.

I remember realizing, in real time, that I wasn't being invited into a future. I was being assessed for one.

It had nothing to do with my actual financial reality. What lingered was the implication beneath it. That before I could be fully chosen, I needed to be considered, measured, and weighed.

Something in me tightened then. Not defensiveness. Not anger. Just a quiet doubt that hadn't been there before.

I felt myself move from partner to possibility, from woman to variable. Like commitment was something I had to qualify for instead of something freely offered.

That shift became unmistakable when he spoke about marriage not as love, but as strategy. He explained that his first marriage had been rooted in love, but that this time, stability was the priority.

I remember how my chest tightened when he said it. Not because financial security isn't important—but because love had quietly been removed from the equation.

In that framing, marriage wasn't about choosing a partner. It was about minimizing risk.

And suddenly, I understood what my body had already been reacting to. I wasn't being loved toward a future. I was being evaluated for usefulness within one.

I didn't challenge it. I took it in. By that point, I had learned how to hold discomfort quietly, how to reinterpret conditional language as patience, how to tell myself not to personalize moments that felt deeply personal.

But my body registered what my voice did not say. Safety was being postponed. Access was already being requested.

And love that asks for openness before offering security is not partnership. It is power dressed as practicality.

When I voiced my truth, the room often turned. I would say, "Even with all the access I have to your world, I don't always feel at home here." The answer was quick: "I always make people feel at home." My reply: "You don't get to tell me how you make me feel."

That's when the tension would crack. Naming my needs was received as an attack on character, and instead of repair, there was retreat. Sometimes even a clean break, like snipping a thread, only to circle back later with a half-hearted, "It's not worth throwing away," but without clarity on what would change.

The truth was, something had been thrown away long before those moments, by the months I spent swallowing my needs to keep the peace. In therapy, Dr. Clark didn't let me sidestep it.

"You talk about what you gave," she said, "but what about what you needed?"

Her question forced me to face the ache I had been carrying. Nights when I longed for comfort but settled for silence, days when my joy had to shrink so his space could expand. Speaking it out loud felt like both a confession and a release: I had been present for everyone else's story but missing in my own.

Dr. Clark leaned forward, her eyes kind but unflinching. "You told him once that you didn't know what was wrong or how to tell him to help you," she said softly. "Do you remember that?"

I nodded, my throat tightening at the memory. "Yes," I said quietly. "I meant every word. I was breaking, and I didn't even have the language for what I needed."

"That moment wasn't weakness," she said gently. "It was truth. You were finally admitting what your body had known long before your mind caught up: you'd been strong for so long, you forgot how to ask for care."

I exhaled slowly, the tears this time not from confusion but from release. For the first time, I didn't just hear her, I felt her. That moment wasn't about him not knowing how to help, it was about me finally realizing I couldn't keep pretending I didn't need it.

That truth wasn't only reflected in therapy. It showed up in the voices of those who loved me most. I remember one evening after dinner with family and friends, the kind of night that should have ended in nothing more than laughter. The air was warm, conversation buzzing like music, plates still scattered with crumbs, glasses half-empty, and everyone leaned back in that comfortable way that comes when you've eaten well and settled into each other's company.

I cupped a warm coffee between my hands, letting the steam rise like a veil, content to sit in the rhythm of easy chatter. That's when my sister-in-law's voice cut through the noise, not sharp, not harsh, but steady and clear enough to still the room.

"You don't even know your worth," she said with a soft tone and a loving smile.

The words landed differently than any critique ever had. She didn't say it to wound me. She said it to wake me. Her eyes held mine as if to say, "Don't forget who you are." Another friend nodded, their face soft with agreement, not in judgment but in solidarity. It wasn't an accusation; it was a reminder. An echo of what my spirit had been whispering all along, but I had refused to hear: I was shrinking again.

The laughter quieted. Even the clink of glasses seemed to pause. For a moment, the room grew heavy with unspoken truths, and I felt exposed, like someone had pulled back the curtain I kept carefully drawn. My instinct was to brush it off, to make light of it, to protect myself with a smile. But my throat tightened. The coffee cup trembled just enough that I set it down before I spilled it.

Inside, a storm rose. Don't they see how much I give? Don't they know what I've sacrificed? But beneath that defensiveness was something else, relief. Relief that someone else saw what I had been afraid to name. Relief that they loved me enough to risk saying it out loud.

I stayed quiet that night, letting their words echo instead of answering. But when I replayed the moment later, I realized it wasn't about them doubting me. It was about them believing I was more than the version of myself I had accepted. They were telling me that where I was, what I was settling for, didn't fit the woman they knew me to be.

And they were right.

Their reminder was both sting and salve. Sting, because it hurt to know I had drifted so far from my own worth. Salve, because it reminded me that I could still come back to it. That night became less about what was said and more about what was revealed: even in my shrinking, others could still see my size. They refused to let me go unseen, even when I was the one dimming my own light.

I had journaled it too, though I didn't always believe my own words. If I ask for closeness, I'm told I'm doing too much. If I ask for support, I'm told I'm making it a thing. What I needed wasn't complicated. But every time I named it, the response came back like a verdict: wrong, heavy, unnecessary.

That's how love becomes conditional. Not because you don't know what you need, but because you start to believe that naming it makes you unworthy.

Even in what was supposed to sound like an affirmation, I was left unseen. When people asked him how we made it, his answer was always, "She knows what she has at home." Never, "We know what we have in each other." Never an acknowledgment that he had a treasure too. And when I questioned it, only then did he backpedal: "I mean, I know what I got too." But that was the problem; if it had been true, it would have been spoken without being pressed. Words given under confrontation don't feel like honor; they feel like correction.

I also had to face a truth about myself: I love out loud. When I choose someone, I choose fully. Loving out loud isn't performance; it's living what's real without shrinking it to make others comfortable. I needed that reflected back.

There's a quiet grief in realizing how often I've edited myself to stay palatable. I softened my voice, made my needs small enough to tuck into a corner. I called it patience; my body called it depletion. Dr. Clark pressed again, "Tanya, what would it look like if you stopped making excuses for what you didn't receive?"

The silence that followed was its own confession. I had been excusing, explaining, and rationalizing. I told myself he was busy, tired, carrying his own load. But beneath those excuses was the truth: my needs weren't invisible. They were ignored.

Therapy later helped me see the pattern for what it was: I had confused endurance with intimacy. I thought being easy to love meant being easy to overlook. That realization stung, because it meant grieving the years I spent silencing myself in hopes of being chosen.

Being resilient means having the ability to adapt, recover, and push through challenges. But resilience should never be mistaken for an open invitation to test someone's limits. It is most often born out of necessity, not choice, a survival instinct, not a lifestyle. I had proven I could endure, but endurance is not the same as being cared for. The expectation that resilient people can "handle anything" too often becomes a silent burden, one that leads to exhaustion, burnout, and even resentment. Strength should not be an excuse for others to disregard my well-being. I realized I was worthy of peace, softness, and spaces where support replaced struggle.

Dr. Clark told me once, "You thought being easy to love meant being easy to ignore. But Tanya, love that ignores your needs isn't love at all, it's convenience."

That landed in my chest like a key turning a lock.

I've always had a nurturing spirit. It's why I became a nurse. Caring for others is my nature, and I don't apologize for that. But I had to learn that giving endlessly without being refilled is not strength, it's depletion. There is a difference between pouring from overflow and pouring from my cup. Overflow means I'm sustained, full, and able to give freely without harm. But when I pour from my cup, I empty myself. And if no one is pouring back into me, there's nothing left.

Friends have told me for years, "Tanya, you have to let people help you. They can't show up if you never let them know." And I did grow. I became better at asking for help, better at receiving. Still, in love, I found myself surrounded by men who seemed to believe my strength was a reason to do less. They mistook my ability to survive as an absence of need. But I wasn't asking for survival—I was asking for partnership.

Invisible sacrifices didn't just exhaust my spirit; they affected my body. Perimenopause amplified that reality. Sleepless nights left me more raw to disappointment. Hot flashes made me crave tenderness, not distance. Mood swings made me long for steady love, not shifting excuses. The absence of care felt louder because my body was already asking for more.

What I know now is this: I wasn't asking for too much. I was asking for presence. For reciprocity. For the everyday care that says, I see you and proves it without being begged. I won't shrink to be loved again. My needs don't make me hard to love; they make me human. And if love can't hold my humanity, it isn't love, it's convenience.

Because reciprocity is more than gestures. It's the difference between being known and being understood. Anyone can claim they "know" you, but too often what they know is only the version of you they've built in their own head. Understanding requires more. It means seeing the whole of me, flaws and all, and still choosing to stand close. It means being loved enough to be held accountable, not dismissed. It looks like action beyond words: showing up in unexpected places, placing me in rooms I didn't know I needed, or calling just to speak life into me. Wanting me to win is one thing. Choosing to show up for me, time and again, that's what understanding looks like. That's where love grows.

Spotlight Reflection

If your love has to whisper to be welcomed, it isn't intimacy, it's invisibility. I think back to that night at the dinner table, coffee cup trembling in my hand, when my sister-in-law said I didn't know my worth. It hurt because she was right in ways I hadn't admitted to myself. My silence wasn't strength; it was me folding small. That moment became proof that invisibility isn't just felt inside, it's noticed outside too.

Unfiltered Moment

They knew my headlines; they never learned my paragraphs. Knowing the "what" is easy. Understanding the "why" requires presence.

Journal Prompts

- Where have I made my needs small so the relationship could feel "easy"?
- What does being "loved out loud" look like for me, and how will I recognize it?
- If I wrote the "Apology That Never Came," what truths would it contain?
- What mantras protect my calm without erasing my truth?

- How does my body react when my needs are consistently ignored, and what practices help me reclaim my voice?
- Where in my life have I been asked to "be strong" when what I really needed was support? How can I begin to create boundaries that honor my peace, not just my resilience?

Once I saw how often I had folded myself small, the only way forward was learning how to unfold, unapologetically.

✍ Journal Here:

____

____

____

____

____

____

____

____

____

____

____

____

____

____

____

Chapter 9

YOUR LITTLE BUSINESS

"Your gift will make room for you and bring you before great men." – Proverbs 18:16 (KJV)

The words rolled off his tongue like a joke, but they landed heavily in my chest. He said it with that half-smile and half-shrug that told me he thought it was harmless. But nothing about it was harmless. My business wasn't little. It was the leap I had taken after walking away from a six-figure salary. It was the dream I stayed up late at night to plan, and the reason I poured myself into rooms where nobody knew my name, but everybody knew my work by the time they left. To call it little was to call me little, and I couldn't un-hear it.

At first, I told myself not to make it bigger than it was. Maybe he didn't mean it like that. Maybe he was just trying to be playful. But playful doesn't minimize your life's work. Playful doesn't make you feel invisible in your own relationship.

What I wanted wasn't complicated. I didn't expect him to run my business, pitch my services, or close deals on my behalf. I only wanted him to open the doors that were already within his reach. That's what partnership meant to me: positioning me so I could walk into the room and do the rest.

He seemed to understand that, at least in theory. He would sit across from me and say it with conviction:

"You know what, I'm going to introduce you to so-and-so. They'd love what you're doing. They've got connections that could really help push this forward."

My eyes would light up. Not because I couldn't find my own way, but because hearing him speak that way felt like pride. It sounded like belief. It sounded like he saw me.

But the introductions never came.

Weeks would pass, and I would circle back, gently, almost apologetically.
"Hey, remember you mentioned connecting me with so-and-so? Do you still think that could happen?"

His body would shift, his tone sharp, his patience evaporating.
"Why are you bringing that up again? Don't you think I've got enough on my plate already?"

It baffled me. He was the one who made the promise. He was the one who put the possibility in the air. And yet, somehow, my reminder turned into pressure, my hope became a fault line between us. The problem wasn't me asking, the problem was his words never matching his actions.

I started paying attention to patterns. Like how I would post about an event, tagging him, giving him shine, while he never once reposted a flyer of mine.

Like how I would talk about him in rooms he didn't even know he had been mentioned in, while my business lived in the shadows of his silence.

One night, after an event I had poured myself into, I went home tired but proud. The turnout was strong, the energy high, the feedback affirming. I opened Instagram, ready to soak in the ripple effect of the night. I checked his page. Nothing. No post. No story. Not even a single picture from the evening he attended. He had been there physically, scrolling his phone in the corner, but his presence never translated into support.

That silence spoke louder than any word he could have said.

During a session in Dr. Clark's office, I finally said it out loud: "He called it my little business."

She tilted her head. "How did that land in you?"

"Like he was shrinking me," I admitted. "Like the thing I left everything for wasn't worthy. And if it wasn't worthy, maybe I wasn't either."

Dr. Clark leaned forward. "What does it mean when someone you love minimizes what gives you life?"

"It means they don't see me," I whispered. "Or worse, they see me, and they don't want me to be bigger than them."

She let the words sit, then asked, "And what truth do you know now?"

I drew a shaky breath. "That my business was never little. That my gift was always making room. His silence wasn't proof that I was small, it was proof that he was threatened."

And here is the truth I see now: saying "I want to see you win" is easy. But real support shows up in action. It looks like introductions that are followed through, not dangled and discarded. It looks like a repost that costs nothing but affirms everything. It looks like being proud enough to say, "That is my woman, she is building something incredible."

I did not get that. What I received instead was jealousy disguised as indifference. When someone sees your light, they either want to amplify it or dim it. And he chose dimming.

But the thing about women entrepreneurs is that we learn resilience in the shadows. We know what it is to be minimized, to be dismissed, to be told our dreams are "cute" or "little." We build anyway. We pitch anyway. We show up in rooms anyway. And every time the door stays closed, we learn to find a window, a side entrance, or to build the building ourselves.

That is what his lack of support taught me: my dream did not need his validation to be real. It needed my persistence, my faith, and my willingness to keep showing up when no one was clapping. The jealousy that tried to shrink me only sharpened me. His silence did not stop my work, it fueled it.

I kept going. And I always will.

Spotlight Reflection: Support Is Action

Support is not about grand speeches or promises that never materialize. It is about alignment between words and deeds. When someone says, "I want to see you win," but does nothing to contribute, no introductions, no encouragement, no amplification, what they are really saying is, "I want the credit for caring, but not the responsibility of showing up."

True support does not compete with your light, it reflects it. It does not shrink your vision, it stretches it.

Women entrepreneurs know this contradiction too well. We are told to "dream big," but treated as if those dreams are hobbies. We are applauded in private and minimized in public. And still, we build. Not because of the applause, but in spite of the silence.

Unfiltered Moment

I remember sitting at my laptop one night after another empty promise. He had told me he would connect me with someone weeks earlier, but when I reminded him, it turned into an argument about how I was "pushing too much." I stared at the screen, the cursor blinking on a flyer I was creating for my next event.

For a moment, I wondered if maybe my business really was small. Maybe I was reaching too far, expecting too much. But then I looked at what I had built: the partnerships, the rooms I had filled, the women and men who trusted me to bring vision to life.

I whispered to myself, "It is not little. You are not little."

That was my truth. Even if he never spoke it, I would.

Journal Prompt

Think of a time when someone minimized your dream or failed to show up for it. How did you reclaim your own belief in yourself? What reminder can you carry with you to affirm that your work is never "little"?

Seeing how easily my work was dismissed made me realize how often I had dismissed myself, shrinking to fit into spaces that were not meant for me. That was a pattern I could no longer afford.

✍ Journal Here:

____

____

____

____

____

____

____

____

____

____

____

____

Chapter 10

SHRINK TO FIT, NO MORE

"Ain't I a woman?" — Sojourner Truth, 1851

Eight years. That's how long I chose myself. Not because I didn't have options, men tried to fill the empty seat beside me. But I knew that seat wasn't meant to be filled just for the sake of saying I wasn't alone. I had already lived that mistake: staying in a situationship that turned into a relationship, even though my spirit whispered it would never grow me. I stayed long past my exit. And when I finally walked away, it nearly broke me.

So, I stayed single. Out of necessity, not fear. Those years became my refining fire: learning me, rebuilding, relocating, and saying no when I knew yes would be too costly. By the end, I wasn't bitter, and I wasn't hiding, I was ready. I had become the woman I wanted to be in love: grounded, open, resilient, soft, and strong.

So, when he came along, I thought: This is it. My chance to give the best of me. And I did. But it wasn't his chance to give the best of himself. My spirit felt it from the beginning, he wasn't ready. Hope made me override my knowing. And slowly, almost without noticing, I started to do the very thing I had promised myself I wouldn't do, shrink.

There is a particular quiet that settles in when you start editing yourself for someone else's comfort. It doesn't arrive with a bang. It creeps. It softens your tone, rounds your edges, and convinces you that smaller is safer.

I didn't start small. I came in whole, laughing loud, loving fully, wearing color and perfume and joy. Somewhere along the way, I started to dim. I gained weight. Clothes I loved stopped fitting. The mirror felt like a test, not a reflection. The people I loved didn't cause all of that, but they didn't help either. Words like "You don't really have to get dressed up" may have been meant as comfort. I heard them as indifference.

I'm not pretending I was perfect. Menopause had me on a rollercoaster: hormones shifting, moods swinging, sleep scarce. Hot flashes made me want to disappear at times, and the absence of tenderness deepened that instinct. Mood swings left me craving stability, but instead I often felt judged for being "too much." Sleepless nights made my resilience thinner, and the absence of empathy cut sharper. My body was already asking for room to expand, but the relationship expected me to contract.

I could be sharp-tongued when hurt. I own my edges. But silence isn't grace, it is distance dressed up. What I wanted was emotional safety. A simple "Owning your own business is scary sometimes. I've got your back." I didn't need a savior; I needed a steady hand and voice. Instead, I was met with logic when tenderness would have carried more weight. There were days when I was already carrying more than my heart could hold, and instead of shelter, more weight was added. Not out of malice. But impact doesn't consult intent.

What I needed wasn't another task or lecture, I needed someone to say, "Not her. Not now. I'll take this one."

And yet, even in those moments, my mother's lessons echoed. She always said it wasn't just what you said, but how you said it. I knew the danger of words spoken in anger, how they can scorch the very earth you may need to walk again tomorrow. So, I tried to pause, hold it, think, reframe, so that my words came rooted in kindness, not fire. Sometimes I succeeded. Other times my hurt slipped past the guardrails. But even then, my compass was clear: never aim below the belt, never let pain turn me into someone I didn't recognize.

One night, the conversation cracked open:

Me: "You keep telling me I'm strong. And I am. But do you realize that using my strength as a reason not to step in leaves me unsupported?"

Him, shrugging: "I don't want to overstep. If you need something, you'll ask."

Me: "That's the problem. I shouldn't always have to ask. If you see me carrying it all, why wouldn't you step in? Why wouldn't you want to?"

That moment sealed it for me. Strength without support is just loneliness dressed up.

Some partners could meet me there. We could disagree without destroying each other. Others only knew how to argue antagonistically, pressing for resolution right then and there, unwilling to honor silence as space to think.

To them, my pause looked like avoidance. To me, it was preservation. That contrast revealed a truth: not everyone argues to resolve. Some argue to win. And when the goal is winning, kindness is dismissed, and you are left defending your character in the fire of someone else's chaos.

Looking back, I can see I was in a kind of functional depression: moving, loving, producing, while a wordless ache pooled underneath. I smiled in photos. I hosted events. I prayed with others. And yet, inside, I was shrinking. When someone won't celebrate your light, you start dimming to match the room.

In therapy, Dr. Clark asked, "When did you first notice you were shrinking?"

I thought for a moment. "When my laughter got quieter. When I started holding back joy so he wouldn't feel overshadowed."

She nodded slowly. "And what did that cost you?"

"Pieces of myself I'll never get back," I admitted. "Confidence. Color. Energy. I was living muted, hoping my softness would make me easier to love."

"Did it work?" she asked.

"No," I whispered, tears stinging. "Because the shrinking never stopped. The goalposts kept moving. And I kept disappearing."

Dr. Clark leaned forward. "That's not compromise, Tanya. That's self-abandonment. And every time you shrank, you taught your body that survival mattered more than wholeness. The grief you feel now isn't just for the relationship, it's for the parts of you that had to go quiet to keep it alive. What do you want to teach your body now?"

That was the language I hadn't yet found on my own: self-abandonment disguised as compromise. Friends reminded me that laughter that feels stifled isn't joy, it is survival. My body reminded me too, through fatigue, fog, and a restlessness that no achievement could quiet. And I grieved not only the relationship, but the parts of myself I had muted to keep it afloat.

What I know now is simple: I don't want a love that needs me smaller to work. I won't keep proving I am worthy of the tenderness I already give. If I am "too much" for the room, I will change the room, not myself.

Spotlight Reflection

When I said, "I need you," and received excuses instead of presence, my body grieved what my mouth kept negotiating. Alignment begins where my excuses end.

Unfiltered Moment

Respect is not only tone, it is timing and responsiveness. The opposite of love isn't hate; it is indifference dressed as logistics.

Journal Prompts

- What is one boundary that, when I honor it, keeps me aligned with the woman I am becoming?
- How will I remind myself that asking for tenderness is not weakness, but a reflection of my worth?

- What signals does my body give me when I begin to dim, and how can I honor those signals without delay?
- When conflict arises, how can I pause for preservation, ensuring my truth is spoken in real time?

Choosing alignment in love taught me how to choose it in work, and in myself.

✍ Journal Here:

Chapter 11

THE BET ON ME

"Sometimes the biggest risk isn't leaving, it's staying where your spirit can no longer grow."

– Tanya Bennett

I spent nearly thirty years in nursing, my name stitched into uniforms, my hands carrying lives in and out of crisis. Steady, respectable, predictable. And yet, a whisper kept rising: "This isn't the end of your story."

Event planning, what began as a side hustle, lit a different part of me: creativity, orchestration, community. I felt alive pulling details together, seeing vision turn into atmosphere, watching people light up inside a moment I had shaped.

A milestone celebration in New Orleans sealed it: second line down the street, horns colliding with laughter, parasols twirling, joy braided into memory, plus a surprise message from a hip-hop legend that set the room ablaze. It wasn't just an event. It was belonging in motion. I knew then: "This is what I'm supposed to do."

So, I leapt and left the pension track for purpose. Some days felt like flight, others like free fall. Through it all, I told myself, "I will always bet on me."

What I didn't expect was how that leap exposed cracks in love. I thought partnership meant presence. Instead, I was met with silence, excuses, and absence.

"I just don't understand why you'd leave something so steady," he said once, shaking his head.

"Because steady isn't the same as fulfilled," I answered quietly.

When I needed encouragement, I got deflection. When I needed a hand, I held my own.

Betting on me sharpened my eyesight. The same clarity that builds budgets and strategies revealed where I was living on credit in love, borrowing hope, carrying the debt of unmet needs, overdrafting my spirit. Some partners liked the version of me who played it safe, who stayed predictable. But entrepreneurship made me unpredictable, daring, risk-taking, fully visible. And when I stepped into that visibility, it revealed who could clap for me in public and who only tolerated me in private.

Launching a business while navigating perimenopause meant my body was also in transition. Sleepless nights made the silence in my relationships louder. Hot flashes in the middle of client meetings tested my confidence, but they also taught me humility and humor. Mood swings stripped my tolerance for half-love and half-support.

"You've changed," one partner said with irritation.

"Of course I've changed," I replied. "I'm growing. Growth isn't betrayal, it's evolution."

I no longer had the capacity to carry both the weight of my changing body and the weight of someone else's inconsistency.

Therapy became my anchor through the leap.

Dr. Clark leaned back in her chair, eyes steady. "What do you feel when you say, 'I bet on me'?"

I exhaled. "Power. Fear. Relief. It's all mixed together. Some days it feels like I'm flying. Other days it feels like I might hit the ground."

She nodded. "And when you hit resistance, from others or from yourself, what does that voice inside you say?"

"It says, 'Maybe you should've stayed. Maybe steady was safer.'"

"But what does your spirit say?" she pressed gently.

I paused, then smiled through tears. "My spirit says, 'This is where you come alive. This is what obedience to yourself looks like.'"

Dr. Clark leaned in. "Then let that voice be louder than fear. Remember, the risk isn't the leap, it's betraying yourself by staying where you no longer grow."

It reminded me that choosing joy isn't selfish, that redefining purpose isn't reckless. Each session gave me permission to trust the whisper, even when fear shouted louder. Therapy helped me see the leap not as abandoning stability, but as stepping into alignment.

And yes, there was grief too. Not just grief for leaving behind a career that had defined me for decades, but grief for realizing that some relationships weren't built to grow with me. "If loving me requires me to stay small, then you don't really love me," I admitted to myself after one particularly raw session. Betting on myself meant losing people who only knew how to love the version of me that stayed small. That loss stung, but it was also a release.

What I know now is that betting on myself didn't just build a business; it built a life. It built me. It revealed who could stand beside me when my spirit expanded, and who only wanted me contained.

Spotlight Reflection

The boldest investments are in yourself. Sometimes the return is clarity about who and what gets to stay.

Unfiltered Moment

From the outside, it looked risky; inside it felt like relief. As I ran toward myself, I noticed who ran with me, and who didn't.

Journal Prompts

- What leap have I delayed because of fear?
- How do my relationships respond when I take risks?
- Where have I been borrowing hope instead of being poured into?
- What proof already exists that I can trust myself?

- If I bet on me today, what is my next small step?

Not everything that shines is safe to hold. Clarity brought me to the edges of the frame.

✍ Journal Here:

Chapter 12

RED FLAGS IN A PRETTY FRAME

"All that glisters is not gold." — William Shakespeare

Sometimes what is dressed in romance is dysfunction in disguise. Red flags do not always scream, they slow-dance in tuxedos, whispering affirmations while editing the truth.

Charm can look like consistency: daily calls, playlists curated for your mood, nightly prayers, and intentional dates. Early on, I believed the picture. Over time, the frame tightened; there were subtle reminders that if the relationship failed, the responsibility would fall on me. It sounded like commitment, but it landed like blame dressed as devotion.

Even the way he spoke about us in public carried an edge I could not ignore. When people asked how we made it, his answer was always, "She knows what she has at home." It was never said with pride in us, only with the weight of what I supposedly owed. It carried an unspoken message: he was the prize, and I should feel lucky. The words landed not as affirmation but as dismissal, stripping away my value in the relationship. When I finally pressed him, he quickly added, "I mean, I know what I got too." But by then, I already knew the correction was not care, it was cover. The disrespect was not in the stumble; it was in the instinct. And I stayed, even as my gut told me otherwise.

Questioning inconsistencies brought defensiveness and distance. Messages got shorter, calls less frequent, accusations sharper: "You're too sensitive." Narrow declarations such as "Men and women can't be friends" felt cynical and small. Control does not always roar. Sometimes it whispers as care: I just like knowing where you are. Sweet at first. Later, surveillance.

Simple truths I named were reframed as character attacks. What I was really touching was not their character, it was their control.

Joy itself could be treated as rebellion. In rooms with music, when I let myself go, danced, laughed, shined, I felt glares instead of shared celebration. If intimacy is supposed to make you more alive, why did I feel like my fullness was a threat?

Even space became a red flag. There was a constant battle over where we spent time, always their home, rarely mine. Excuses sounded noble: "I just don't stay at anyone else's place." But that resistance said more than presence ever could.

Because how can you truly know me if you never see me in my own world? How can you understand the way I move, the rhythms of my day, the small comforts that make me who I am, if I am always in your space, adjusting to your comfort zone?

The true essence of a person is often revealed in their sanctuary. And if you never step into mine, you never really see me, you only see the version of me that exists inside your frame.

Future talk sounded expansive until I added action. I researched. I strategized. I dreamed aloud. But when I did, the tone soured. It wasn't a partnership that was desired, it was an echo.

I softened. Second-guessed. Shrunk. Red flags didn't come as explosions; they came as small edits to me. A mention of an ex's family member still lingering too close. Strategic introductions that looked like access but felt like management. My aloneness in a crowd where I was supposed to feel chosen.

After having dinner, I named it: how often I tiptoed emotionally. The reply was quick: "You're always trying to find a problem." The ride back was silent. In it, I asked myself a question that would not leave me: Who am I becoming to make this work?

Ignoring red flags became almost impossible. I didn't have the energy to keep excusing neglect. Lies sound different when you finally stop rehearsing hope.

Eventually, I just got tired. Tired of crying. Tired of circling the same hurt, the same disappointment. Not because I thought he had stopped caring, but because I finally knew I deserved more, better. And the truth was undeniable: my happiness, my joy, my destiny, those belonged to me. That shift didn't erase the pain, but it gave me the strength to stop excusing it.

I remember once blurting out, almost to myself: "I don't want to keep proving I can survive him."

The room was quiet for a beat before my therapist responded gently but firmly. Dr. Clark tilted her head, eyes steady. "Why do you think you said that out loud?"

I swallowed hard. "Because survival is not love. Survival is just survival."

She leaned forward. "And what did you call survival before?"

"Commitment," I whispered. "Loyalty. Strength. I thought lasting was proof of love. But all it proved was how much pain I could tolerate."

Dr. Clark's voice softened but stayed firm. "Tanya, endurance isn't intimacy. If love requires you to shrink, that's not partnership, it's performance. And every time you accept it, you're rehearsing heartache. What do you want to rehearse instead?"

Tears welled. "Joy. Peace. The kind of love that makes me more alive, not less."

That clarity landed deep. I had mistaken endurance for intimacy, resilience for partnership. I thought lasting was proof of love, when in reality, all it proved was my tolerance for pain. Grief still came, but this time it didn't hollow me out, it sharpened me. It carried the lesson I had refused to face: what I allow will continue.

What I know now is that love isn't proven in appearances, it's revealed in patterns. And any relationship that requires me to shrink to survive will never be love, no matter how pretty the frame.

Spotlight Reflection: Listening the First Time

I remember the day one of them looked me straight in the eye and said, "Let me show you who I really am. I ain't shit. I ain't never gonna be shit. You deserve better than me."

My young ears didn't hear it for what it was. I translated his confession into a wounded plea: He just doesn't believe he deserves a love like mine. I can prove him wrong. I told myself I could show him that everybody deserves good love.

But the evolved me, the woman I am now, understands something different. He wasn't seeking reassurance. He was revealing himself. He was telling me exactly who he was, and I refused to listen. I created a softer story in my mind, one that aligned with my hope instead of his reality. And because I didn't listen, I invited heartache I could have spared myself.

It wasn't until I stopped rewriting his words, until I let myself truly hear them, that I saw them for what they were: not insecurity, but declaration. He showed me who he was. And when I finally chose to understand, I realized the lesson wasn't about him at all, it was about me listening to the truth the first time it's spoken.

Unfiltered Moment

Shrinking to keep the peace erodes the very connection you're trying to protect. Without authenticity, love becomes performance.

Journal Prompts

- When have I ignored a red flag because it was wrapped in charm or consistency?
- Where did I excuse control as care?
- What parts of me did I silence in the name of love?
- What does discernment feel like in my body, and how will I trust it sooner?

Once I named the red flags, the question underneath them finally had room to speak.

✍ Journal Here:

Chapter 13

WAS IT LOVE OR JUST ACCESS?

"Access to me is not the same as intimacy with me." — Author Unknown

A slow morning, nothing planned, the kind that should feel warm and easy. Conversation thin, eyes elsewhere, presence without engagement. It wasn't cold. It wasn't warm. It was nothing. The echo of a pattern: closeness when it was convenient, distance when it required intention.

Light shone when my presence saved him effort, then dimmed when it meant showing up for me. Pride stayed silent, even when it mattered. There were suggestions, but rarely a full presence. I didn't need applause; I just needed signs of true partnership.

That was the distinction: knowing versus understanding. Someone can know your favorite flower and still not grasp why it matters when it is given. Someone can sit in your company and still not feel you. Knowing is surface; understanding is soul.

I remember asking him once why he was with me. His answer came quickly, almost too easily: "Because I can learn from you."

It didn't feel like love. It didn't even feel like admiration. It felt like an assignment. His words disturbed me from the beginning because they revealed exactly how he saw me, not as a partner but as a resource. A place to draw from. A woman he could study, absorb, and benefit from.

And a quiet fear settled in me: What happens when he no longer needs what I give? What happens to us when I'm no longer useful?

That fear never left. It lived underneath every moment when my presence was valued more for what it offered than for who I was.

"But I'm here, aren't I?" he said once, as if proximity was proof enough.

"Being here isn't the same as being with me," I replied. "Access to my time doesn't mean intimacy with my spirit."

There was also the imbalance of space. They took up room in my world, while I was rationed in theirs. Sometimes there was even reluctance to step into where I lived, into the rhythms of my sanctuary. But if you never enter my space, how do you learn the essence of me, the way I rest, the way I create, the way I breathe when I'm home? Without that, all you have is performance.

The clearest pattern revealed itself in effort. Whenever I felt most connected, it was usually tied to my giving: time, energy, presence, and flexibility. In contrast, the return was often scheduled around convenience. Access was offered more freely than intimacy.

So I faced the question I had been avoiding: Was it love, or was it access? Realizing it was access, not love, meant grieving. Grieving a relationship and the years spent proving I was enough. I had to mourn the part of me that shrank to stay chosen, settling for tolerance over celebration. Leaving was more than walking away: it was admitting my investment was misplaced. That loss needed honoring. Love as access meant losing both a person and my story about us.

"You're making this more complicated than it has to be," he argued when I tried to explain.
"No," I said softly, "I'm finally telling the truth. There's a difference between having me and holding me."

Therapy helped me distinguish feeling from fear. I feared being too much, but the truth was I gave too much for too little. Naming access broke the illusion that convenience could replace care. The work was clear: stop confusing proximity with partnership.

In one session, Dr. Clark asked quietly, "What does intimacy feel like to you?"
I thought for a long moment. "It feels like presence, not just in the room, but with me. Noticing when I'm tired, celebrating when I win, sitting with me in silence without making me feel alone."

She nodded. "And what did you settle for instead?"
"Proximity," I admitted. "He was there, but not with me. He had access to my life, my body, my time, but never my spirit. And I let myself call that love."

Dr. Clark leaned forward. "That's not love, Tanya. That's attendance. And attendance isn't intimacy. Why did you accept that trade?"

Tears stung as I answered. "Because I thought being chosen in any capacity was better than not being chosen at all."

Her voice softened, but her eyes held mine. "And what do you know now?"

I inhaled deeply. "That being tolerated is not the same as being treasured, and I deserve to be treasured."

I always knew that love was a choice, but time and experience gave me deeper clarity. I whispered once, more to myself than to him, "You have to choose me, too." Love requires you to choose to stay in it. You have to choose that person every day. You have to choose to take the good with the bad, the sunshine with the storms. When one person stops choosing, the weight falls unevenly, and no matter how much you give, you can't hold up a love that has already been put down.

Access isn't intimacy. Presence without praise, care, or reciprocity is an empty room with the lights on. Now I see: my worth isn't defined by someone's convenience, but by how steadfastly they remain when it isn't easy.

Spotlight Reflection

Sometimes the loudest answer is the quiet exchange, when your presence is valued more than your person. That's the moment to choose your worth.

Unfiltered Moment

Access isn't intimacy. Presence without care or reciprocity leaves the room empty.

Journal Prompts

- Where have I mistaken access for love?
- Did I confuse intimacy with mere proximity, and was I cherished for who I am or only valued for what I gave?
- What does feeling seen, not just accompanied, look like for me?
- If I stopped doing, who would still choose me for who I am?
- What boundary protects my energy from transactional connection?
- What grief am I still carrying for the illusions I once called love?

✍ Journal Here:

____

Chapter Echo: Closing Part II — The Unseen and Unsaid

Echoes don't lie. They return the truth of what was said and what was lived. For too long, I mistook proximity for partnership. But echoes have a way of revealing emptiness: what's hollow, what's lacking, what was never really there. And in that hollow space, I finally heard myself.

PART III: THE RECLAIMING

Clarity became my compass, and from that moment on, I chose truth over tolerance.

Chapter 14

FROM TOLERANCE TO TRUTH

"You teach people how to treat you by what you allow, what you stop, and what you reinforce."
— Tony Gaskins

For years, I confused endurance with love. I told myself that if I just held on long enough, through the silences, through the sharp tones, through the weight of unmet promises, things would eventually turn in my favor. I thought love meant pushing past discomfort, swallowing my words, and staying quiet so I would not rock the boat.

But what I tolerated became the very thing that stripped me down. Every moment I allowed disrespect to pass unchecked chipped away at my own self-worth. Every excuse I accepted, every silence I filled with my own rationalizations, was a betrayal of myself in the name of preserving "us."

The truth is, what I was calling love was really a cycle of survival: a cycle of diminishing myself just to keep someone else comfortable, a cycle of thinking loyalty meant abandoning my own needs. That was not love; it was fear dressed up as devotion.

Healing cracked that pattern wide open. Therapy, journaling, prayer, and reflection gave me language for what I had been feeling but could not yet articulate. They gave me clarity on the line between grace and self-betrayal.

They helped me understand that love is not meant to break you down; it is meant to build you up.

There was a moment in therapy when my counselor leaned in and asked softly, "Why do you equate silence with peace?" The question stopped me cold. I fumbled for an answer, finally admitting, "Because speaking up always seemed to make things worse." She let the silence hang before asking again, "But did it make you better?" That question followed me out of her office and into my journal that night, where I wrote for hours, letting the truth bleed onto the page.

In another session, Dr. Clark pushed me further. "What do you think silence really bought you?" she asked.

"Time," I answered. "The illusion of harmony. A few days without tension."

Her eyes narrowed slightly. "But did it buy you love?"

Tears filled my eyes. "No. It bought me distance. It bought me resentment. And it bought me the slow unraveling of myself."

Dr. Clark nodded. "Then the silence was never peace, it was a transaction. And you paid with pieces of yourself. What would it look like if your voice became your boundary instead of your burden?"

I whispered the words as if I was hearing them for the first time: "It would look like freedom."

And once I saw it clearly, I couldn't unsee it. I could no longer excuse what cut me down or silenced my spirit. So, I started to name what I would no longer compromise. Not preferences. Not wish lists. Non-negotiables.

My Five Non-Negotiables

1. **Respect** — I will never accept derogatory, belittling, or demeaning talk. Not from anyone. My parents never spoke to me that way, and no one else will either.
2. **Fidelity** — Don't cheat on me. If you no longer want to be here, walk away. But don't strip me of my dignity.
3. **Individuality** — I am a whole person on my own, and I expect the same of my partner. We create a life together as individuals, not as halves searching for completion.
4. **Faith Alignment** — God is central to my life, and I need a partner who honors that alignment with me.
5. **Communication & Safe Space** — We must be able to tell each other the truth, even the hard truth, without fear. Safety in communication is not optional, it is foundational.

Naming these truths wasn't about building a wall, it was about setting a standard. It was about honoring myself enough to say, "This is what love must look like if it is to live here."

The evolved me understands what the younger me couldn't: that I am not here to prove my worth through suffering. I am here to be loved in a way that protects my dignity, nurtures my spirit, and aligns with the fullness of who I am.

There were nights I lay next to someone and felt completely alone. Nights where words meant to love me left me bleeding instead. And I told myself to be patient, he would change. I told myself this is just a rough season. I told myself not to make it worse by speaking up.

But here is the truth I can no longer deny: I stayed because I thought my silence would buy me love. I stayed because I thought proving I could endure made me worthy. And the hardest part to admit? Deep down, I knew I was settling for less than I deserved.

The realization came quietly one morning as I stared at my reflection in the mirror: If you keep shrinking, who will you even be by the time he finally notices you? That thought cut deeper than any argument ever had.

I am no longer willing to pay the price of tolerance. My love will never again be a bargaining chip exchanged for scraps of respect.

Spotlight Reflection, The Cost of Tolerance

Every time I accepted less than I deserved, I trained someone to believe that was enough. I confused endurance with love and silence with peace. But silence does not heal, it erases. Love is not proven by how much pain you can carry. Love is proven by how well it honors your dignity.

Unfiltered Moment

I used to think silence was strength. Now I know it was fear.

I used to think endurance was loyalty. Now I know it was self-abandonment.

I used to think waiting would earn me love. Now I know it only delayed my freedom.

Journal Prompts

- Where in your past have you tolerated something that went against your inner truth?
- What lesson did that tolerance teach you about yourself?
- Write down your top three non-negotiables. Why are they important to you, and how will they protect your future self?
- How can you create a safe space to honor your needs in current or future relationships?
- What does respect look like to you in action, not just in words?

Clarity became my compass, and from that moment on, I chose truth over tolerance.

✍ Journal Here:

____

____

____

____

____

____

Chapter 15

THE CONVERSATION THAT CHANGED EVERYTHING

"When someone shows you who they are, believe them the first time."

— Maya Angelou

In the weeks before, my journal had become my confessional. I noticed the energy shifting, the conversations thinning. I asked about it and was met with vague reassurances: "I'm trying to figure some things out." Exactly one week before, I wrote a prayer asking God to step in, fix it, dissolve it, whatever His will was, because I couldn't keep carrying the weight of uncertainty. I didn't realize then that my prayer was already setting the stage for what was to come.

It started with a whisper through someone else, not directly from the person I loved. Word that my travel or work schedule had become too much. I felt stung, but also hopeful. I reminded myself of an earlier gesture that had once felt like trust, symbols of openness that convinced me we were building something real.

I chose to show up in person, carrying hope and intention. I didn't bring just myself. I carried small tokens of care, reminders of what I thought mattered to us both. My prayer was simple: let this soften us, let this bring us closer.

I had no idea that showing up would unravel everything.

At first sight, there was no smile, no warmth, only distance dressed in silence. The greeting was sharp, dismissive anger standing where tenderness should have been. My presence wasn't received as love. It was treated as an intrusion.

What unfolded wasn't a conversation, it was control. Sharp words framed as principle. Anger masquerading as honesty. My care was recast as desperation. My effort twisted into offense.

I said simply: "If someone had shown up for me, I would have seen it as love." But the reply wasn't openness, it was a doubling down, always keeping the upper hand, even in hypotheticals. That was when it clicked: this wasn't about us; it was about power.

Every effort I made was reclassified as too much. Every attempt at closeness became evidence against me. I could stand right there, heart wide open, and still not be seen. The silence that followed wasn't empty, it was clarifying. This wasn't miscommunication, it was the truth revealed.

As I left, I carried the weight of clarity more than the weight of loss. Later, I returned what had once symbolized belonging, an item that had meant access and openness at the start. In the end, it represented only an illusion. Sending it back was my way of releasing not just the object, but the false story it carried.

I wasn't angry when the door closed. I wasn't even heartbroken. I was grieving: grieving the version of myself who had stayed too long, the energy

I poured into proving my love, and the illusion that this was ever a partnership. Menopause made that grief heavier: restless nights, the exhaustion of carrying both emotional and physical weight. Therapy gave me language for it. Grief wasn't weakness, it was a boundary forming. It marked the end of shrinking, the end of negotiating my worth, the end of explaining myself into exhaustion.

Afterward, therapy with Dr. Clark:

"So, tell me again what happened when you showed up," Dr. Clark said, her tone steady, not rushing me.

I exhaled. "I thought I was showing love. I thought being present would speak louder than any words. But instead of being received, I was treated like I had crossed a line."

"And how did that feel?"

"Like my presence was a crime. Like I had to defend why I cared, why I even showed up. I kept thinking, if someone had done this for me, I would have seen it as love."

Dr. Clark leaned forward. "But Tanya, love doesn't punish presence. If your care was turned into offense, that's not a boundary, that's avoidance. Do you see the difference?"

I sat quietly. The word avoidance landed like a sharp edge cutting through fog. "So, it wasn't me being too much?"

Hearing it put words to the ache I felt standing in that room. I wasn't being met with honesty. I was being managed, controlled, and diminished.

"No," she said firmly. "It was him showing you what he could not give. And your body knew it. That's why you've been carrying grief. Not because you lost love, but because you finally believed what it revealed."

Tears pricked my eyes. "So grief isn't weakness?"

"Grief is boundary-forming," she answered. "It's your spirit saying: this far, no further. You asked God for clarity. This was your answer."

I whispered it back, almost to myself: "This was my answer."

She paused, then added, "Tanya, have you thought about why he could celebrate showing up for others, but punish you for showing up for him?"

I frowned. "Because it made no sense. I was the one who told him presence mattered. I encouraged him to fly home to see his niece, and he cried at his bedside. But when I did the same for him, I was treated like I was out of line."

"That's because it wasn't about presence, it was about control," Dr. Clark explained. "When you encouraged him to go to his family, he could still believe the choice was his. But when you showed up for him, your love arrived on your terms, not his. And that threatened his control."

Her words sank like stones in water.

"And there's projection too," she continued. "He could give presence, but he couldn't receive it. Receiving meant admitting he needed it. And for someone who equates strength with independence, need feels like weakness."

I swallowed hard. "So, he wasn't rejecting my care, he was rejecting being seen."

Dr. Clark nodded gently. "Exactly. Being seen without permission exposes what he'd rather keep hidden. What you offered as care, he experienced as exposure."

The irony pierced me. I had taught him to show up, but when I lived out that same truth toward him, he resented it.

I journaled after therapy: I was done playing by rules I hadn't written. I didn't lose that day, I found myself. I found the part of me unwilling to barter presence for punishment, unwilling to confuse silence for safety. Writing it down helped me honor the clarity for what it was, not rejection, but revelation.

Spotlight Reflection: Presence Without Permission

What he once called love, he later labeled intrusion. The irony was sharp: the wisdom I gave him for his family was the same truth he rejected when it was turned toward him.

Sometimes the resistance isn't to the act of love itself, it's to the vulnerability it demands. To receive without asking requires surrender, and surrender feels unsafe to those who cling to control.

But love is not about control. Love is about care. True care cannot always wait for permission.

Unfiltered Moment

I thought I was showing love.
Instead, I was shown the truth.
That was the day I stopped begging to be received and started demanding to be respected.

Journal Prompts

- When have you been punished for showing up in love?
- What are your non-negotiables for emotional safety?
- Where have you accepted behavior you now know was unacceptable, and how would you handle it differently now?
- When have you prayed for clarity and received an answer that wasn't what you hoped for, but exactly what you needed?
- How might you honor your own prayers by trusting the clarity God has already revealed to you?
- What grief have you carried for the illusions you had to release?

I walked away not defeated, but clear. The clarity I prayed for was the freedom I needed. From that moment on, my choice was simple: stop shrinking where God had already told me to stand tall.

✍ Journal Here:

Chapter 16

BECOMING ME AGAIN

"And still, I rise." — Maya Angelou

I walked away from a relationship I loved, one I once thought would last. It wasn't easy. Love doesn't just dissolve because you recognize something is no longer serving you. My heart still ached even as my spirit whispered, "This is not where you belong."

Leaving meant stepping into loneliness and uncertainty, but it also meant stepping into freedom. I relocated to another state, not for anyone else, but for me. For growth, for breathing room, for rediscovery.

The first night in my new space, I sat surrounded by half-open boxes, silence pressing in from every corner. For the first time in a long time, there was no voice telling me what I was or wasn't doing enough of. Just me. I remember whispering into the quiet, "God, what now?" The answer didn't come in thunder, it came in stillness. Slowly, I began to breathe again.

In that season, I got to know myself in a way I never had before. I wasn't just my parents' daughter, my brother's sister, or my daughter's mom. I was me, a woman who had dreams, flaws, triggers, and desires of her own.

"Who are you outside of everyone else's needs?" Dr. Clark asked me one afternoon.

I hesitated, then admitted, "I don't know. I've always answered to those roles first."
She gave me a knowing smile. "Then maybe this season isn't about loss at all. Maybe it's about finding the woman who's been waiting under all those titles."

Therapy became my companion again. I sat with my triggers instead of running from them. I studied my reflections in the mirror of memory and asked hard questions: Where did I lose myself? Where do I begin again?

Menopause was part of that rediscovery, too. The weight gain, the sleepless nights, the unpredictable moods reminded me that my body was changing as much as my heart. Instead of resenting those changes, I began to see them as another way my body was asking me to pay attention. Healing wasn't only emotional, it was physical too.

But life doesn't hand us transformation in a straight line. I entered another relationship. My gut told me early it wasn't working, but I ignored myself. I silenced the voice that had warned me before. Slowly, I began to shrink, to bend, to compromise myself into shapes that felt smaller than who I was.

That shrinking turned into anger, anger at him, yes, but more so at myself. Because I knew better. I knew when it was time to go, but I stayed anyway.

"How many times will you betray yourself, Tanya?" I wrote in my journal one night, tears dripping onto the page. "How many signs will you ignore just because you're afraid of starting over again?"

I discussed my journal entries with Dr. Clark during my next session. She leaned forward, her eyes steady. "Why do you call it betrayal instead of a mistake?"

"Because I knew," I whispered. "I knew the red flags. I felt the tightness in my chest. I heard the warnings in my own spirit. And I still stayed."

Her voice softened. "So, the betrayal wasn't his, it was yours against yourself."
Tears rolled down my cheeks. "Yes. That's what I can't forgive."

She paused, letting the silence hold me before asking, "What would forgiving yourself look like?"

I shook my head. "I don't know yet."
"Start here," she said gently. "Name the truth without judgment. You ignored yourself, but you also found yourself again in that very breaking. That's not weakness, it's wisdom earned."

Grief surfaced in that season too, not just grief for a relationship ending, but grief for the ways I kept betraying myself. I grieved the years of second-guessing my worth, the times I believed endurance proved love. But grief, even in its ache, became a teacher. It showed me what I could no longer accept.

Still, there's grace even in anger. Anger told me I was worthy of more. Anger told me I had betrayed my own intuition, and in naming that, I could finally honor it again.

"You're too hard on yourself," a close friend told me over coffee.

"No," I said quietly, "I'm finally being honest with myself. I knew better. I just didn't trust myself enough to act on it."

She reached across the table and touched my hand. "Then maybe trusting yourself again is the real becoming."

She was right.

And so, I built new rhythms for my life. Healing wasn't only in therapy sessions or late-night journal entries. It became the rituals I chose every day.

I started rising earlier, sometimes at 5:30 A.M., sometimes closer to 6:00 A.M., just to meet myself before the world rushed in. The first thirty to sixty minutes became sacred: no phone, no email, no scrolling. Just prayer, gratitude, and affirmations whispered into the morning stillness: You are worthy. You are enough. You are loved. You are still becoming. At first, it felt strange to hear my own voice declaring what my heart struggled to believe, but over time those words rooted themselves in me.

I committed to moving my body again. I created a plan to work out at least four days a week for an hour, sometimes in one stretch, sometimes split into two thirty-minute intervals. It wasn't about chasing perfection, it was about honoring consistency. Each drop of sweat reminded me: You are strong. You are still moving. You are here.

I returned to the simplest ritual of peace: walking outside. I took short breaks during the day just to step out, to feel the sun, to hear the crunch of gravel or the rustle of leaves. Those walks became my communion with God, my conversations with nature, my way of remembering that I was part of something bigger.

I drank more water, not because someone told me to, but because my body deserved replenishment. I gave myself ten to fifteen minutes of quiet every day: no music, no TV, no phone. Just me. Just presence. Those moments reminded me that my own company was enough.

Each ritual became its own declaration: I am worth this time. I am worth this care. I am worth listening to.

This chapter of my life wasn't about failure. It was about awakening. Walking away, moving, rediscovering, shrinking, getting angry, grieving, creating rituals, all of it led me back to one truth: I am allowed to choose me.

What I know now is that leaving isn't weakness, it's clarity. What I know now is that choosing myself is not selfish, it's sacred. And every time I honor my intuition, I honor the God in me who always knew the way forward.

Spotlight Reflection: Trusting Myself Again

Walking away is not weakness. It is strength in disguise. Sometimes the bravest act of self-love is saying, "This no longer fits who I am becoming."

Unfiltered Moment

I didn't fail because I left. I failed the moments I stayed when I already knew the truth. Becoming me again meant forgiving myself for ignoring my own voice and finally trusting it enough to lead me forward.

Journal Prompts

- Think back to a time when you felt yourself shrinking.
- What signs did you ignore?
- How would trusting yourself fully have changed your choice?
- What small steps can you take today to remind yourself you are worth listening to?

What began as walking away became walking back into myself, and that journey demanded I release the shame I had carried far too long.

✍ Journal Here:

____

____

____

____

____

____

____

____

____

____

Chapter 17

NO MORE SHRINKING, NO MORE SHAME

"And the day came when the risk to remain tight in a bud was more painful than the risk it took to blossom." — Anaïs Nin

For years, I made myself smaller. I squeezed into spaces never meant to hold me, trying to be digestible for people who had no appetite for my truth. I dimmed my light to keep others comfortable, ignored my intuition to keep the peace, and convinced myself that love required sacrifice, even when the sacrifice was always me.

At first, shrinking felt like survival. If I softened my tone, swallowed my hurt, and pushed down my needs, maybe things would be easier. But every time I made myself smaller, I chipped away at my own brilliance. Shame lived in the corners of those compromises, whispering that I should have known better, that I should have left sooner, that I should have demanded more.

But shame doesn't get the final word. Not anymore.

I now see shrinking and shame as two sides of the same coin. Shrinking agrees with the lie that you are "too much." Shame agrees with the lie that you are "not enough." Both rob you of the truth: you are already whole, already worthy, already enough.

Part of that shrinking came from the changes in my body. Menopause layered itself over grief and exhaustion, making me question my worth in new ways: weight I didn't recognize, moods I couldn't always manage, a mirror that didn't reflect the woman I used to know. For a while, I believed the lie that these shifts made me less lovable.

"Maybe if I lose the weight, maybe if I act lighter, maybe if I stop being so sensitive…" I'd catch myself thinking. But each 'maybe if' was just another way of saying I wasn't enough as I was. Deep down, I knew that wasn't true.

They were never evidence of deficiency, they were signs of a body in transition, still worthy, still mine.

The turning point came when I decided I was done apologizing for my fullness, done explaining away my needs, done carrying someone else's discomfort as if it were mine to hold.

No more shrinking. No more shame.

That night, when the door clicked shut behind me, it wasn't dramatic. Just a soft close that whispered: I'm done here.

I stood in the stillness, luggage untouched, shoes still on, and realized I didn't need him to understand me. I only needed to understand myself. Strength without self-respect isn't strength at all, it's survival. And I was tired of surviving love that didn't feel like love.

I sat down and mentally stacked the evidence:

- The promises that went unkept.
- The moments my vulnerability was met with suspicion instead of care.
- The way my boundaries were treated like an inconvenience.
- The routine of contact without the consistency of effort.

In therapy, I gave those bullet points words. Dr. Clark asked me, "Do you see the difference between patience and self-abandonment?" I sat with that question, rolling it around my heart like a stone. For years, I had mislabeled waiting as loyalty, silence as peace, and endurance as strength. Now I knew better.

Therapy reminded me that boundaries are not rejection, they are clarity. And clarity is love.

If love is supposed to be safe, why did I spend so much time in defense mode?

That night I made a quiet decision:

- No more explaining myself to be believed.
- No more dimming my joy to avoid someone else's insecurity.
- No more apologizing for the kind of love I give.

I grieved the years I spent thinking disappearing would keep me loved. But grief also carried a gift: it taught me that nothing is wasted if it brings me back home to myself.

This wasn't about revenge. It was about release. And release, I realized, is its own form of freedom.

The next morning, sunlight poured through the blinds. Maybe it was the same light as before, but I saw it with new eyes. I brewed coffee, sat with my journal, and wrote one bold sentence:

"I will never again be punished for showing up."

Then another:
"The right person will never require me to shrink."

I used to think I had to ration my love as if it might run dry. But the problem was never the amount of love I had to give, it was who I was giving it to.

With the wrong person, my love became labor: emotional presence without reciprocity, support without return, sacrifice without care. I carried discouragements that weren't mine, helped rewrite narratives, poured affirmations into someone else's dreams, all while remaining unseen.

With the right person, love will feel like sunshine, not a spotlight they want to escape. My showing up won't be questioned, it will be welcomed.

So, I made myself a promise:

No more shrinking. No more shame. I will stand in my fullness, and those meant for me will recognize it as a gift.

What I know now is that shrinking is not humility, it's self-erasure. What I know now is that shame has no authority over my worth. I am not too much, and I am not hard to love. The moment I choose to stand in my fullness without apology, I already win.

Closing this chapter wasn't just about reclaiming my voice, it was about preparing my heart for the truth that love was never supposed to hurt like that.

Spotlight Reflection: Standing Tall

To shrink is to deny your own existence. To carry shame is to live under a weight that was never meant for you. Freedom begins the moment you decide you are worthy of taking up space, worthy of being seen, worthy of being heard, exactly as you are.

Unfiltered Moment

I am not too much. I am exactly enough for the love that is aligned with me.

Journal Prompts

- Where in my life have I been shrinking to fit someone else's comfort?
- What shame have I carried that doesn't belong to me?
- What does it look like for me to take up space without apology?
- What boundaries can I set to protect my full self in love and friendship?
- How would my relationships shift if I refused to shrink ever again?

Reclaiming my fullness meant more than speaking louder, it meant unmasking the parts of me I had hidden, even from myself. The work ahead was not about others, it was about telling the truth about me and daring to finally unmask myself.

✍ Journal Here:

Chapter 18

UNMASKING MYSELF

"Your pain is the breaking of the shell that encloses your understanding."
— Kahlil Gibran, The Prophet (1923)

For so long, I wore masks I didn't even realize I had put on: masks of strength when I was weary, masks of patience when I was hurting, masks of grace when I was quietly disappearing inside myself. Reclaiming my fullness meant stripping away those layers. Unmasking wasn't about exposing myself to others, it was about finally telling the truth to me.

There was a season when the only honest thing I could do was cry. Not because I was weak, but because my body needed a way to let the truth out.

I cried for the times I didn't trust my gut.
For the red flags I excused.
For the moments I let the praise of others outweigh what I already knew deep down.

Some nights, I blamed myself for weeks on end. I told myself I should have known better, I should have listened sooner, I should have left earlier. But grief isn't logical, and neither is love. Everything collided at once: the loss of loved ones, the strain of family transitions, the challenge of building a new business. The ache layered itself, and my heart had to hold all of it at the same time.

Layered on top of all of it, my body shifted with menopause. The weight, the mood swings, the sleepless nights, all of it was part of the ache I carried. My heart wasn't the only thing holding too much, my body was speaking too.

"God, how much more can I hold?" I whispered into the dark one night, pillow damp with tears.

And yet, beneath every wave, I knew I was resilient. I knew God would steady me. I knew grace would meet me where I was.

So, I started where I could: with accountability that didn't sound like punishment. I owned the sharp edges of my tongue on hard days. I owned how grief and hormonal shifts altered my moods. I owned that sometimes I was vocal and it didn't land well. None of that excuses disregard or disrespect, it simply names my humanity. I can be accountable and still refuse mistreatment. Both can be true.

Therapy gave me a new language: for boundaries, for ownership without over-responsibility, for honoring what belongs to me and releasing what doesn't. Dr. Clark told me, "You can apologize for your part without carrying someone else's patterns." That one sentence shifted me.
I could love without normalizing the ways others numb, whether through distraction, denial, or avoidance. My peace is not collateral.

I also stopped asking, "Why didn't I see it?" and started asking, "What do I do now that I do?" That shift saved me.

I began tending to my spirit like a home worth living in. Some mornings, I rose early to pray before touching my phone. Other days, I journaled without editing, letting the pen carry truths I couldn't yet say aloud. I walked in nature, letting wind and sunlight unclench what grief had tightened. I called friends who told me the truth with care, and when their voices weren't enough, I let my mother's voice ground me. I let silence do its work. I let myself feel without apologizing for feeling.

Grief was part of my unmasking too. It came in waves: the grief of lost time, of versions of me that stayed too long, of dreams I had to release. Instead of resisting it, I let grief wash through, knowing it was clearing space for something truer.

And I started forgiving. Not because I forgot. Not because what happened was small. But because I deserve lightness. I deserve a life not tethered to someone else's unhealed parts. Forgiveness became a decision to stop rehearsing the pain and start rehearsing my peace. It was boundaries with softness, truth without bitterness, trusting myself when my spirit said "no," and honoring myself when my spirit said "go."

I'm not a scorned woman.

I'm a learning woman.

And learning looks like loving myself enough not to abandon myself again.

There was a time I mistook self-abandonment for kindness, calling it patience or grace. I saw the best in people long after they showed me their worst. That was not compassion, it was me leaving myself behind. Now I know better. And knowing better means choosing myself every single time.

I still deeply believe in partnership: the kind that shows up, repairs without punishment, and delights in each other's becoming. But now I believe in it with boundaries. If loving you means disappearing, I'm no longer interested.

Unmasking myself wasn't a single moment, it was a process: a shedding of old stories, misplaced loyalties, the belief that shrinking made me worthy, and the shame that menopause made me unlovable. I didn't go backwards. I was tested forward. Life handed me a lesson dressed in familiarity so I could finally choose myself: clearer, stronger, and without apology.

What I know now is that unmasking isn't about exposure, it's about alignment. The more I told the truth about myself, the more I remembered that I am not broken, I am becoming. And every time I listen to my own voice, I honor the woman I was always meant to be.

Now, I stand with the same heart but a stronger spine. Still loving. Still soft. But never again small.

Spotlight Reflection: The Kindest Truth

Healing is telling the whole truth about yourself without hating yourself for it.

Unfiltered Moment

I didn't fail because I felt deeply.

I failed myself by ignoring what those feelings were trying to tell me.

Now I listen, and I move accordingly.

Journal Prompts

- Where have you called self-abandonment "kindness"?
- What does compassionate accountability look like for you, language that is both honest and gentle?
- Write a vow to yourself that begins, "I will no longer abandon myself when…" Then list three actions that honor that vow this month.

Unmasking myself showed me the cost of silence and self-abandonment. The next lesson was even clearer: real love was never supposed to hurt like that.

✍ Journal Here:

____

Chapter 19

LOVE WAS NEVER SUPPOSED TO HURT LIKE THAT

"Love is supposed to be a soft place to land, not a battlefield to survive." – Author Unknown

There's a kind of pain that doesn't scream. It lingers, quiet, constant, and heavy. That's what our love became: something that chipped away at me while wearing the mask of connection.

I used to believe love meant sacrifice. That if I kept showing up, kept giving, kept staying, it would eventually be enough. But I learned that being available doesn't mean being seen, and being loyal doesn't guarantee being loved in a way that feels like home.

There were good moments, and that's what made it so confusing. Concerts where we danced like nobody else existed. Evenings with music playing low in the background. Kitchen trivia games that ended in laughter. Spontaneous slow dances next to the stove. Conversations about marriage. Introductions where I was called "the one." In those early days, I believed it. I wanted to believe it.

But love isn't built on moments. It's built on consistency, honesty, and unconditional care.

Over time, those small omissions began to reveal a deeper truth. A simple gesture like flowers, something I had named as meaningful, was withheld again and again. The absence wasn't about money or access; it was about intention. Love listens. Love remembers. Love follows through.

"I don't understand," I said once quietly. "Why is it so hard to do the thing you know makes me feel seen?"

His reply was sharp and dismissive. "You're making too big a deal out of it. They're just flowers."

But they were never just flowers. They were the difference between being considered and being ignored.

Then there were slips of the tongue, moments where I realized that even in closeness, I was carrying someone else's ghosts. Instead of being fully seen, I became a mirror reflecting back insecurities and comparisons I never asked to hold.

My love was interpreted as pressure. My vulnerability was treated as criticism. My attempts to repair were framed as attacks. Logic was offered when tenderness was needed. Deflection replaced accountability. The result was a slow erosion of safety.

The breaking didn't come from a fight. It came from the silence, the way my feelings were dismissed before they were even fully spoken, the way my joy was dampened, my boundaries brushed aside, my presence mistaken for permanence.

"Why does it feel like I have to defend why I want to be loved?" I wrote one night, the pen heavy in my hand. "Why do I feel lonelier next to him than I do when I'm alone?"

Love isn't supposed to feel like walking on eggshells. It isn't supposed to feel like decoding riddles or questioning your worth in the presence of someone who claims to love you.

But I stayed. I kept trying. I kept praying. And in that trying, I lost sight of myself.

Menopause made those silences feel heavier. Sleepless nights blurred into tired mornings, and the changes in my body left me more vulnerable to the sting of being unseen. It wasn't just emotional depletion. I felt it physically: hot flashes during tense conversations, fatigue after another disappointment, the deep ache of a body and heart both carrying too much.

Therapy helped me untangle this. It showed me that what I mistook for patience was often self-abandonment. Dr. Clark leaned in once and said, "Endurance without reciprocity is not partnership, Tanya, it's depletion." Her words echoed in me like a bell. Therapy gave me tools to name my needs without apology and to separate endurance from intimacy. In that space, I began to see that survival mode is not the same as love.

And yes, I grieved. I grieved the years of giving without reciprocity, the pieces of myself I muted, the belief that if I could just hold on long enough, care would eventually show up. That grief wasn't wasted; it cleared space for the truth that love should never require me to erase myself.

What I know now is that survival can mimic love if you let it, but it's not the same. Endurance doesn't equal intimacy, and silence is not peace. What I know now is that love should steady you, not strip you. It should expand you, not erase you. And if I ever feel myself shrinking again, that's my cue to walk away, not dig deeper.

Spotlight Reflection: The Truth in the Silence

Sometimes the deepest heartbreak isn't found in the arguments but in the quiet, in the way you stop sharing your feelings because you already know they'll be dismissed, in the way you shrink, not because you want to, but because you're tired of fighting to be heard. That's where the breaking happens, in the silences that speak louder than any words ever could.

Unfiltered Moment

Love was never meant to feel like confusion, doubt, or exhaustion. It was never meant to demand the erasure of self. Looking back, I see how many times I muted my own needs, how often I mistook endurance for devotion. But endurance isn't love, it's survival. Survival should not be the standard in a relationship.

Journal Prompts

- Where in your life have you confused survival with love?
- What small moments of silence or dismissal have felt louder than arguments?
- If love is meant to be your soft place to land, what does that look and feel like for you now?

I had given love every chance, even when it left me weary. Naming the truth that love was never supposed to hurt like that was painful but also freeing. Now it was time to reclaim what had always been mine: my voice, my worth, my story.

✍ Journal Here:

____

____

____

____

____

____

____

____

____

____

____

____

Chapter 20

I AM THE STORY

"I am deliberate and afraid of nothing." — Audre Lorde

If there's one thing I refuse to surrender, it's my belief in love. I have bent, I have broken, I have healed, and still, I rise with tenacity. The wounds were real, but they will never rewrite who I am. My resilience is not just survival, it is vision. I can see the love that's meant for me because I never stopped looking with a whole heart.

I know what I deserve now: a love that chooses me daily, on the bright days and the hard ones, when I am soft and when I am still learning my edges. A love that honors my voice, protects my peace, and holds the line with me when storms come. That's not fantasy, that's alignment.

Some people do hurtful things, but not everyone is a hurtful person. I choose to keep my lens clear. I choose to keep my heart open. I choose to believe that someone equally self-led will find me where I am and stay, because we both choose it, again and again.

"I am not too much. I am not hard to love." I repeated those words in the mirror until my reflection believed them. What once sounded like wishful thinking became a declaration. I wasn't waiting for someone else to validate me. I was telling the truth back to myself.

My strength is not in how long I tolerated misalignment. My strength is in how fully I trust myself now. I am resilient. I am tender. I am hopeful on purpose. And when the right love arrives, it will not ask me to shrink to fit. It will expand with me.

Looking back, I see the truth clearly now. I gave fully, I loved deeply, and I carried more than was ever mine to carry. But the clarity I hold today is freedom. I know I am not too much and not hard to love. I choose myself. I choose my worth. I choose my voice.

In that choice, I reclaim the truth that I am not the side story, not the supporting role, not the background character in anyone else's narrative. I am the story. Whole. Worthy. Unashamed.

One morning, after everything had unraveled, I stepped outside before dawn. The air was cool, the sky not yet awake. I stood there barefoot, feeling the ground steady me. "This is it," I whispered. "This is where I begin again." In that quiet, I realized I wasn't waiting for love to find me. Love was already in me, steady, rooted, rising.

When the dust of everything I survived finally settled, I stood not as what was lost, but as what was found, me.

Resilient Light

I have a spirit that refuses to dim, even when life has tried to weigh me down. My resilience isn't just about survival, it's about transforming pain into purpose, challenges into change, and dreams into tangible realities for myself and for others.

I shine, but my light isn't harsh or blinding, it's warm, guiding, and affirming. I lift others as I climb, offering both compassion and leadership.

At my core, I am deeply rooted in faith, purpose, connection, and legacy, driven not just by ambition, but by a sincere calling to heal, build, and leave an impact that outlives me.

If I distill it even more simply:
I am a vessel of faith-driven resilience, love, and purpose.

Spotlight Reflection: Choosing Myself

The greatest story you will ever tell is the one you live. Not the story of who left, who stayed, or who failed to see your worth, but the story of how you rose, reclaimed your voice, and chose yourself.

Unfiltered Moment

I am not what was done to me.
I am what I choose to do with it.
And in choosing myself, I became the story.

Journal Prompts

- Where in your life have you played the supporting role in someone else's story?
- What words of truth do you need to repeat to your reflection until you believe them?

- How can you practice choosing yourself daily in small, consistent ways?
- What parts of your past need to be reframed as lessons, not labels?
- If you were to write one sentence today that begins your next chapter, what would it be?

✍ Journal Here:

CHAPTER ECHO: CLOSING PART III - THE RECLAIMING

"I am guided by character and anchored by intuition. I see beyond the surface, hear what isn't said, and read the room's quiet truth. I love myself, wounds, scars, and all. And I choose me." — Tanya T. Bennett

Conclusion

STRENGTH THROUGH STRUGGLE

"Out of difficulties grow miracles." — Jean de La Bruyère

Life has a way of chiseling us, like stone sculpted by water over time. The same currents that could drown us also shape us, smoothing edges, revealing form, and uncovering strength that has always hidden beneath the surface.

My struggles became my sculptors. Grief, heartbreak, menopause, entrepreneurship, betrayal: they were not weights meant to sink me, but tools that carved me into someone new. Each blow hurt, but each cut revealed another layer of resilience.

I once feared that all the loss would break me, but it didn't. Instead, it broke me open. It made space for more faith, more compassion, more clarity. The cracks became windows where light could enter.

I am not the same woman I was when this journey began. I carry scars, yes, but also wisdom. I carry the echoes of what I survived and the proof that I am still standing.

Strength, I learned, isn't loud or boastful. It's quiet, steady, like roots deepening underground while the storm rages above. My strength was born not in avoiding struggle, but in walking through it, barefoot and trembling, until I found solid ground again.

And now, I know. I am not defined by what I lost. I am defined by what I refused to let go of: my faith, my dignity, my story.

This is my story of strength through struggle. But more than that, it is my story of becoming, unapologetically, unshakably, and undeniably me.

Epilogue

THE MIRROR DOESN'T LIE

"She is clothed with strength and dignity, and she shall rejoice in time to come."
—Proverbs 31:25 (KJV)

There's a moment after the breaking when you realize the world did not end, it widened. The noise quiets, the ache settles into something named, and you start hearing your own voice again. Not the one that bargained for peace, but the one that remembers who you are without convincing anyone else.

I once thought closure came from an apology, a final talk, a tidy bow. Now I know closure is a decision: to believe what was shown, bless what was learned, and walk forward without dragging the past as proof. He was the lesson. I am the story.

The mirror taught me this: love is not performance, access, or potential. It is presence. It is reciprocity. It is safety and truth-telling, even when your voice shakes. It is being loved out loud and in the quiet, without disappearing to earn it.

I did not write these pages to put anyone on trial; I wrote them to put my heart back in my own hands. Life doesn't arrive in neat chapters, it comes in echoes. If you recognized yourself here, let it be an invitation, not an indictment. An invitation to set a boundary, start a conversation, seek help, or step into the healing.

I do not regret loving. I regret the ways I abandoned myself to keep love from leaving. That difference matters. Because the woman I am now does not bargain with her worth. She believes in herself for the first time. She names what she needs without apology. She chooses peace, even if it looks like starting over.

Some nights, grief was a room with no doors, loss stacked on loss, memory cutting and comforting in the same breath. But even there, God was present. Proverbs 3:5–6 became less a verse on a wall and more a rhythm in my feet: trust, lean not, acknowledge, and watch the path appear. And it did, one brave, ordinary step at a time.

If you're reading this with a sore heart, I am reaching for your hand across these pages. Here's what I know now:

- You are allowed to want what you want.
- You are allowed to require what keeps you well.
- You are allowed to leave what won't love you in your language.
- You are allowed to be adored without auditioning.

And when the old tapes play, the ones that say you're too much, too sensitive, too needy, remember: "Too much" is what people call women who finally stopped starving.

The life ahead of me is not a reaction to what hurt, but instead, it's a return to what's true. I will dance when the music finds me. I will build work that honors my gifts. I will keep a home where tenderness is fluent and laughter is frequent. I will cherish friendships that clap in the dark. I will love again, sober, steady, equal. Or, I will love my own company with a joy that makes solitude feel like a sanctuary.

The mirror doesn't lie, but neither does hope. Both tell the truth about who I am now: a woman who learned, who stayed soft without breaking, who tells her story in daylight.

If you need a permission slip, consider this yours:
Go where your peace is.
Keep your bright.
Choose yourself on purpose.

And when you meet your reflection tomorrow morning, say it out loud with me:

I am the story.

A NOTE AFTER YOU FINISH

***

This is not the end.

It is a reminder.

You are not too much.

You are not hard to love.

You are worthy of choosing yourself, again and again.

When you feel the urge to shrink, stand taller.

When shame whispers, answer with truth.

When grief lingers, let it teach you, not define you.

Carry this with you:

The story is not what broke you.

The story is how you rose.

And you are the story. Whole, worthy, unashamed.

Go in your becoming.

ABOUT THE AUTHOR

***

Tanya T. Bennett is a writer, entrepreneur, and former Registered Nurse with nearly 30 years of service in healthcare. She is the founder of PUSH 365 Event Group LLC and the Hot Flashes & Cool Conversations Foundation, two brands rooted in her passion for connection, healing, and women's empowerment. A 2022 Chicago Defender Woman of Excellence honoree, Tanya has been celebrated for her leadership, service, and unwavering commitment to uplifting her community.

Through her foundation and wellness advocacy, Tanya hosts powerful conversations about menopause, creating safe, evidence-based spaces for women to learn, share, and navigate this transformative stage of life together. Her voice is trusted, compassionate, and grounded in lived experience.

Tanya's journey from nursing to entrepreneurship reflects her devotion to authenticity, purpose, and legacy. As a mother, daughter, sister, and friend, she draws inspiration from the roles that have shaped her deepest truths. In her memoir, she opens her heart with honesty, offering readers a story of resilience, awakening, and reclaiming one's power.

www.ingramcontent.com/pod-product-compliance
Ingram Content Group UK Ltd.
Pitfield, Milton Keynes, MK11 3LW, UK
UKHW021909190726
13853UKWH00002B/585

9 798218 869489